THE
CASH FLOW
CONTROL GUIDE

Methods to Understand and Control the Small Business' Number One Problem

Second Edition

David H. Bangs, Jr.

UPSTART PUBLISHING COMPANY, INC.
The Small Business Publishing Company
Dover, New Hampshire

About the Author

David H. Bangs, Jr., is founder of Upstart Publishing Company, Inc. He is author of *The Business Planning Guide* (which has sold over 300,000 copies), *Start Up Guide, Managing By the Numbers, The Personnel Planning Guide,* and *The Cash Flow Control Guide.*

Prior to founding Upstart, Mr. Bangs honed his business management and communication skills. He was coordinator of the Business Information Center in Exeter, New Hampshire, a pilot project for a Federal Reserve Bank of Boston regional economic development plan. For several years, Mr. Bangs was a commercial loan officer at Bank of America in Los Angeles, where he worked with small high-tech businesses. At the University of New Hampshire, Mr. Bangs taught courses on logic and the philosophy of science. He is a frequent speaker and acknowledged expert on small business management topics.

Mr. Bangs lives in Portsmouth, New Hampshire with his wife, Lacey, and his black lab, Thud.

Published by Upstart Publishing Company, Inc.
A Division of Dearborn Trade
12 Portland Street
Dover, New Hampshire 03820
(800) 235-8866 or (603) 749-5071

Neither the author nor the publisher of this book is engaged in rendering, by the sale of this book, legal, accounting or other professional services. The reader is encouraged to employ the services of a competent professional in such matters.

Library of Congress Catalog Number: 86-51601
ISBN: 0-936894-02-4

Printed in the United States of America
10 9 8 7 6

For a complete catalog of Upstart's small business publications, call (800) 235-8866.

Table of Contents

Page

To the Reader

Your business' staying power depends on maintaining a positive cash flow: Money has to come into the business at least as fast as it goes out.

This challenge confronts all small-business owners.

Sometimes the problem is simple liquidity. When there isn't enough money to meet current bills (including payroll and taxes), accounts receivable may be the problem. Every account receivable is a cost to you—in effect, you are financing your customers.

Sometimes the problem is chronic, caused by lagging sales or by insufficient capital, and results in excessive borrowing needs.

Sometimes the problem is caused by slipping margins: Cost of sales goes up, contribution to overhead and profit goes down.

Sometimes the problem is seasonal. Inventory purchased for resale may have to be paid for before the selling season. The terms your suppliers demand may be expensive for you to meet, so you don't take advantage of discounts.

Sometimes explosive growth is the problem. Sales become cash more slowly than you plan—so while sales are skyrocketing, so are your cash disbursements. Keeping the two in balance calls for more capital, or more debt, or both.

How do you figure out what to do? Cash flow problems are complex and affect all of us. Most can be solved by taking careful, thoughtful precautions. And if cash flow problems can't be avoided altogether, they can be foreseen, and their impact on your business' survival and profitability minimized.

That's what the *Cash Flow Control Guide* is about. We used a real-life example, drawn from a going business that has had its normal share of cash flow problems. Finestkind Seafoods, Inc. is representative of other small businesses. They have to profitably turn inventory to keep going. They have to watch costs, establish budgets, face unexpected hurdles—and still meet their fixed costs and payroll in a timely way.

To make the best use of this book, modify the worksheets in the text to suit your own business, since the examples drawn from Finestkind (see Appendix One) probably won't reflect the realities of your business. You have to tailor your forecasts, budgets and financial statements to your own needs—perhaps with the help of your accountant, business counselor, or banker.

Follow the steps in the text and you will learn a cash flow control process. The benefits of learning this process are great. Profits will increase because your costs are lower. You will have less need for debt—but have credit available for liquidity needs if and when they arise. You can take discounts and avoid late payment charges. You can avoid cash flow crises—and be able to take advantage of opportunities as they present themselves.

The process is well-proven in practice. We use it at Upstart. Finestkind uses it. And so do thousands of other small businesses. It takes application and patience—and your knowledge of how your business works.

David H. Bangs, Jr.
Portsmouth, New Hampshire

Foreword

Upon completing my first reading of the *Cash Flow Control Guide*, I was struck with one thought: "How many times during the past ten years could I have used the information presented in this book. I learned these techniques the hard way—by making mistakes which, in some cases, could have cost me the company."

In any company, large or small, cash is the fuel needed to generate business. In fact, every major step taken by the small-business owner, whether it is borrowing to support growing receivables or signing a lease on new manufacturing equipment, ends up with a decision to "bet the business." Unless there is adequate information available to support these decisions, your odds of making the right decision may be better at the racetrack.

In my experience, many business owners manage their affairs by the "seat-of-the-pants" approach. If there is money in the bank, something must be going right; if there isn't, it is time to cut back. This approach tends to work well in a stable environment, when sales are relatively steady and costs seem rational, even if they are not always in control. However, when the business environment undergoes changes, the "seat-of-the-pants" approach can make you sit down quickly.

For instance, a rapid sales growth in most businesses, no matter how well accomplished, causes a debilitating cash outflow every bit as difficult to deal with as that caused by operating losses. The typical result of this scenario is a fast unprepared trip to the bank for a short-term loan to tide the business over until sales turn to cash. The problem is that even a banker may not understand the cash flow problems caused by rapid sales growth, and will assume that new sales are going to vanish in a pool of bad debts or that they don't exist to begin with. To avoid these kinds of problems, make sure you have a well-thought-out, long-term financing plan. Your banker and CPA can help you put it together.

The only way to win at the cash flow game is to understand how your business is doing, accurately predict your future capital requirements, and then follow the plan you develop to meet those requirements. The information in the *Cash Flow Control Guide* will help by showing you the techniques used by financial managers in companies ranging in size from those who keep their bookkeeping records in a shoe box to publicly-held corporations. Some of the techniques are not easy; you may have to get professional help in order to implement them. However, there is no substitute for them.

The first financial goal most of us set for our business is to create sustained growth and profitability. This cannot be done without understanding both the opportunities and the limitations we face every day as business owners and managers. This book will not help you uncover opportunities, but if you find them, it will help you plan around your limitations.

Neil C. Herring
Senior Director of Business Development
Damon Corporation Medical Services
Needham Heights, Massachusetts
April 1987

Introduction

Managing for cash flow is managing for survival. Manage cash flow effectively, and your business works. Costs are in order. Sales and collections efforts work together. Margins are protected, market share grows, and profits increase.

Manage cash flow effectively, and your business works.

Mismanage your cash flow, and you won't be able to do much more than struggle to stay afloat and sing the cash flow blues.

What causes cash flow blues? There are four major causes:
1. Fixed costs creep upwards;
2. Variable costs slip out of control;
3. Sales don't turn into cash fast enough;
4. Inventory becomes bloated.
There are other causes—but these are the main profit killers.

This book outlines the steps you can take to improve a less than optimal cash flow. The steps involved are neither magical nor mysterious nor even new. They take time and effort—but they work. In the appendix of this book, you will see how budgets, taken from an actual business, work.

Keep the prime aim—survival—in focus at all times. If gearing up for anticipated sales could lead to financial disaster, take your time. You can't afford to acquire excessive plant and inventory or to hire people too soon. Wait. Wait until your plant is bursting at the seams, your employees are beginnning to pile up overtime, and the sales are there. Then you can expand. Not before.

Cash Flow Has to Be Managed

Start to manage your cash flow by looking at your past performance. Unless you have good reasons to expect differently, expect your business to repeat the same general patterns year after year. Your business has a momentum that's hard to change, and while you can make substantial changes for the worse very easily, making changes that improve profitability is very difficult.

Forecasts and Budgets

Forecasts and budgets are so closely related that they can't be separated. Your forecasts become your budgets. To make budgeting and forecasting simpler, break them into a series of small steps.

1. What are your sales goals? You need these for the budget period and beyond. Sales drive your business. In the long run, operating profits (sales less expenses) are far and away the most important source of cash for your business.

The Difference Between Cash and Working Capital

Cash is the most liquid of all your current assets. It's what you use to pay all your bills.

Working capital, on the other hand, is those current assets left over after all current liabilities are met. Look at your company's balance sheet. Your current assets are listed in order of decreasing liquidity: Cash, Accounts Receivable, Marketable Securities, Notes Receivable, Payments Due From Officers, and so on. Simply stated, a cash flow problem arises when you have current liabilities to meet but no cash on hand: You can't pay bills with accounts receivable.

There are three ways to deal with a working capital problem:

1. Get new, permanent investment (equity) in the business. This solution is most desirable since it does not involve any interest expense. In addition, it solves the number-one small-business problem: undercapitalization.

2. Borrow against accounts receivable. You can take on short-term debt (for one year or less) without incurring excessive interest payments. (The rule of thumb is that the shorter the term of the loan, the lower the interest expense.) This debt is liquidated by the business' inventory turnover.

3. Get a long-term working capital loan. This kind of debt is paid out of profits over three or more years. However, there are two considerations you must keep in mind: The rate of interest will be higher; this type of loan becomes another fixed expense, thereby increasing your liabilities.

Your goal of improved profitability will only be reached by improved cash flow. Ultimately, you must weigh the advantages and disadvantages of each of these three approaches and decide which one (or ones) will work best for you.

---

2. What will your expenses be? You have to meet your fixed costs every month. Other expenses and costs are tied directly to sales, and can be figured as a function of sales level.

3. What's going on around you? General business and economic conditions in your market area or in your target markets, competition, new technologies, and shifts in market taste are among the many variables you have to accommodate. You want your projections to help you set accurate goals, but those goals have to be achieved in the real world. The real world is fickle, imprecise, and has a way of tripping up the overly optimistic forecaster.

4. How do you establish budgets? Companies without budgets invite disaster, and usually get it. Anyone can set up a budget. The trick is to set up budgets that are worth following. A cash flow budget based on your business, your products, your markets, and your experience is going to be worth following. This book can help you set up a cash flow budget that works.

5. How do you use the cash flow budget? Once you have established forecasts, goals and budgets, keep on top of what the business is really doing as compared to what was forecast and budgeted. You put your budget to work through deviation analysis, a simple tool that helps you spot dangers and opportunities early. If you see a trend developing before your competition does, or plug a cash flow leak by noting an expense nudging upward, you will come out ahead.

Work with Your Banker

If you aren't comfortable preparing financial statements, or if you just want to improve your banking relationships, involve your banker in your long-range planning efforts. Bankers are like anyone else: They like to use their skills. Since most bankers have sophisticated financial management skills, it is to your advantage to make the first move. Invite your banker to help you.

Level with him or her. If you keep communications flowing, you will increase the probability of getting the financing you really need, when you need it, and at the lowest cost.

Chapter One:
Determine Your Financing Needs

At some point, no matter how carefully you monitor your cash flow, you will have to borrow: to cover a temporary cash flow gap, to grab an opportunity, or to provide working capital for growth without diluting your equity.

Plan ahead. A written financing plan—whether for a bank's or your own use—is a major step in the right direction. Accurate cash flow projections are integral parts of your financing plan. They help you avoid cash flow problems, anticipate financing needs (for growth or survival), and help you keep your borrowing costs as low as possible.

Your cash flow projection will help you provide clear, factual answers to questions such as:
1. What are my financing needs?
2. Why can't they be met from retained earnings?
3. Are operating profits going to be sufficient to meet long-term debt repayment schedules?
4. How much do I need? When do I need it? Under what terms?
5. Should I use new debt, or is new equity investment needed?
6. How will this loan—if made—be repaid? (Or, from an investor's perspective: How will this investment be profitable?)

If the answer to your financing needs is new or increased bank debt, you must be able to show that you can service the loan from operating profits. One of the classic ways small-business owners trip themselves up is to use this year's financing to pay off last year's debts and operating losses. This kind of pyramiding is devastating. It creates a monstrous debt load that can overwhelm profitability and keep you behind the eightball. That's dispiriting, discouraging, disheartening and disastrous.

How Do You Put Together a Financing Plan?

Start by identifying the different needs for funds. Some of these needs can be covered by operations. Those that cannot (or cannot without tripping you into illiquidity) should be carefully scrutinized to see whether they are necessary. If they are necessary, you can turn to the question of whether or not more debt should be sought—or if the need might be met in some other way.

It's important to remember that if debt financing is needed to cover a cash flow gap caused by insufficient operating profits, the underlying cause must be identified and dealt with before financing will do any good. Borrowing to paper over an operating problem always leads to a worsened situation, tempting though it may be at the time.

Suppose, for example, that your sales have fallen off and costs have risen, making it clear that soon you will have a severe liquidity or working capital

One of the classic ways small-business owners trip themselves up is to use this year's financing to pay off last year's debts and operating losses.

1

problem. If the lag in sales can be cured without borrowing, fine. You can almost always take costs down a notch or two. If you will still have a cash flow problem, then make sure that borrowing won't make it worse. If the sales problem can't be resolved, sooner or later you'll be back to the bank to borrow more, thus driving costs even higher. Your fixed costs are made bigger, increasing the operating loss, so the need for more debt money becomes more pressing.

And so it goes.

Make sure that you know your needs before going to the bank. Your banker will want to know what benefits the new debt will bring. Any banker you'd want to work with will ask, almost before you sit down, what you need the money for and whether you could raise it from operations. To stammer and admit you hadn't looked for operating economies and profits as a way to generate cash is a sure way to lose credibility.

Avoid this. Enter the bank well prepared.

Five Questions Your Financing Plan Should Answer

Your cash flow projection will provide most of the information necessary.
1. *What do you need the loan for?* Is it for working capital? New equipment? Expansion?
2. *How much is needed?*
3. *How will the money be repaid?* Document with cash flow and income projections, balance sheets, and substantial marketing and sales plans.
4. *When is the money needed?* Timing is important. You can often reduce borrowing needs by rescheduling. Some loans (such as those for real estate, major equipment, or any large sum that has to go to a loan committee) take time to process.
5. *What kind of financing is most appropriate for your business? Why?*

Figure 1.1:
Basic Rule of Finance

The basic rule in financing is: *Match the term of the loan to both the term of the need and the source of repayment.*

The use of short-term debt to finance long-term needs cripples a lot of businesses. Using a 90-day note in lieu of permanent financing is very risky. Not only is there the ever-present danger that the loan will not be renewed (bank examiners always flag "evergreen" notes), but there is the added disadvantage of never being able to plan more than 90 days ahead.

1. Short-term needs call for short-term loans (including revolving credit lines).
2. Medium-term needs usually call for term loans.
3. Long-term needs call for both long-term debt and increased equity investment.

Five Types of Financing

Legitimate financing needs fall into five related categories. At any one time you may need recourse to several of these. A going business with a new division is like a startup—it may have working capital needs and will have additional equipment demands.

1. Startups. A new business needs a combination of invested capital and long-term debt. Capitalization needs are detailed in the income and cash flow projections. Trade or industry figures (available from your banker) give an idea of average capitalization needs. Initial equipment and other fixed asset costs can be spelled out in great detail. The balance of debt to equity is important—too much debt too early makes future financing hard to come by.

2. Working capital shortages. After initial capitalization, working capital is generated from operating profits over a long period. If you suffer from chronic working capital shortages due to undercapitalization but are making some operating profits, then the answer may be a term loan. However, you must demonstrate that the loan will more than repay itself in additional operating profits. Quite often, a modest working capital loan will put a business over the hump and provide enough breathing room to make much higher operating profits. You model the impact of the loan in your cash flow projections.

But remember: A working capital loan, which is paid back monthly over a period of three to seven years, adds substantially to your overhead costs. If your business won't generate sufficient added operating profits to cover the loan payments plus 50% to 100%, then added equity is needed, not another loan.

3. Equipment and other fixed assets. Equipment and other fixed asset loans are clear examples of matching a loan to the need and repayment base. Since these loans are ordinarily secured by the equipment, the anticipated useful life of the equipment becomes a major factor in the credit decision.

A very rough guideline is that you can finance equipment with a projected useful life of 10 years for up to 70% of its life, and for as much as 90% of its value. Manufacturers tend to have fairly generous credit policies—but even so, you should follow these guidelines for your own safety.

Don't buy fixed assets on short terms. The timing is wrong. If you are trying to finance your business with sweat equity, fine. This isn't the best place to put sweat equity to work. Finance it for five instead of seven years, or three instead of four.

While equipment loans rarely go beyond seven years, commercial real estate often is financed over 15 or more years, depending on the situation. Since you build equity in equipment and real estate over a number of years, from profits, you want to finance it the same way.

4. Inventory; seasonal progress. These loans are short-term and are usually tied to a clearly defined source of repayment, such as one inventory turn, the fulfillment of a contract, or the sale of a specific asset.

Don't buy fixed assets on short terms.

For long-term credit, a business must demonstrate the ability to consistently generate profits.

Short-term notes are repaid from short-term sources that are clearly identified before the credit is granted.

Medium- and long-term debts, on the other hand, are repaid from less directly identifiable sources. A banker looks to proven management ability (usually evidenced by a profitable history and clearly understood plans) for repayment. Since there is no one fast source of repayment, the risk is greater, and the decision more difficult.

This is a crucial distinction. A company may be an excellent short-term credit risk, but for long-term credit, a business must demonstrate the ability to consistently generate profits.

Remember: Term loans come due every month or quarter, adding to fixed costs. As the overhead rises, so does the risk and the need for more careful management. Your banker recognizes this. So should you.

5. Sustained growth. The final major category of bankable loans is for growth, which can outstrip working capital. A business anticipating fast growth should also anticipate a lot of danger.

As sales go up, liquidity goes down. Sales don't turn to cash as fast as suppliers need to be paid. As you add staff, productivity plummets. New, larger space is needed, with more administrative burden and increased fixed costs. It's inevitable.

The usual solution is a combination of new invested capital, lines of credit tied to receivables and inventory, and long-term working capital loans.

Notice what this implies. If you plan to grow, you must plan to generate profits consistently, at the same time keeping your business liquid to meet current obligations.

To make sure that you maintain liquidity, you have to make sure of your financing. The answer? A financing plan based on thorough income and cash flow projections.

Chapter Two:
Prepare Sales and Expense Forecasts

Cash flow control starts with sales and expense forecasts. These provide the basic data for both income and cash flow projections, which are the primary budgeting tools.

The simplest approach is to extrapolate current sales, using historical financial data as a guideline. The problem with such an approach is that it doesn't take change into account—and if you can count on one thing, it's that business situations change constantly.

A better technique involves breaking your goods and services into several product lines, then using Figure 2.1: Sales Forecasting to arrive at a "most likely" figure.

Begin by assuming the worst. In the column headed "low," put down the sales you'd expect if everything went wrong—poor weather, loss of market share to a new competitor, your star salesperson going to your most hated competitor (taking along his or her accounts), new product competition you can't match, and so on.

Then—this is more fun—assume that everything works out the way you wish. Put down your rosiest hopes in the column headed "high." All your promotional efforts will succeed, markets will grow explosively, your competitors will stub their toes and slink away from the market, your suppliers will fill your inventory requirements instantaneously.

Realistically, sales will end up in between the high and low estimates. The figures here will (usually) be more accurate than a one-time estimate will be. More thought has gone into their preparation.

If you can count on one thing, it's that business situations change constantly.

Figure 2.1:
Sales Forecasting

Sales forecast for the period: _____ to _____ .

Sales	Low	Most Likely	High
Product 1:			
Product 2:			
Product 3:			
Product 4:			
Total Sales:	_____	_____	_____

Expense Forecasts

You can use the same three-column process to forecast expenses. Most expenses are reasonably stable within a sales range.

However, a better approach takes some more subtle distinctions into account.

Expenses fall into two categories: fixed and variable.

Fixed expenses are independent of sales levels (within limits: See Figure 2.2). If sales dramatically increase, some of these expenses will explode. This "step function" is unusual, though. If you anticipate large sales increases, you need professional advice from your banker and accountant to forecast expenses.

Figure 2.2:
Sales and Expenses

Increased sales and increased expenses go together. But not in a smooth line, particularly in growing businesses. If you expect a substantial increase in sales over the next budgeting period, try to figure out what this will mean in terms of:

Operating margins. Will they remain stable? Go lower? Higher? Why?

Fixed costs. New plant and equipment may be needed. What will happen to overhead and administrative expenses? Will new debt be needed?

Profitability. What will the increase do—will there be a lag? What about credit and collection expenses? Bad debt expense?

Expenses, both in absolute dollars and in management time, tend to rise in steps, not smoothly, as a percentage of sales. A modest increase in sales may greatly increase profits, because it won't affect fixed expenses. But a major sales increase can actually result in lowered profits—and severely (if temporary) negative cash flow—if fixed expenses take an upwards leap.

Variable costs rise and fall with sales levels, and can usually be forecast as a percentage of sales. Your own records, plus trade figures, will give you a realistic percentage range for each variable expense.

A very few expenses are mixed. Take a conservative approach and treat these as fixed expenses, unless you have good reasons to link them more closely to sales.

Figure 2.3:
Fixed and Variable Expenses

Fixed Expenses:

Salaries	_____
Payroll Tax	_____
Benefits	_____
Rent	_____
Utilities	_____
Licenses and Fees	_____
Insurance	_____
Advertising	_____
Legal and	
Accounting	_____
Depreciation	_____
Interest	_____
Maintenance and	
Cleaning	_____
etc.	

Variable Expenses:

Sales Commissions	_____
Sales Tax	_____
Boxes, Paper, etc.	_____
Travel	_____
Entertainment	_____
Freight, Cartage	_____
Overtime	_____
Bad Debt	_____

Mixed Expenses:

Telephone	_____
Postage	_____
etc.	

This is not an exhaustive list. If you are undecided about which of your expenses are fixed and which are variable, check with your accountant.

Now list your expenses and "most likely" sales forecasts from Figures 2.1 and 2.3 on Figure 2.4: Sales and Expense Summary. These are gross figures, which will be broken down more finely in the next chapters.

Figure 2.4:
Sales and Expense Summary
One-Year and Three-Year Sales and Expenses (total for each product line)

	Next Year:	Three Years:

Sales: (List your sales figures from Figure 2.1)

1.

2.

3.

4.

Expenses: (List your expenses from Figure 2.3)

1.

2.

3.

4.

Chapter Three:
Prepare Income Projections

You build your income projections on the forecasts you just finished.

Income projections show your anticipated revenues, expenses, and profits. They also include non-cash expenses, such as amortization and depreciation, and show only interest paid on debts. Cash-flow projections, on the other hand, show cash actually received and disbursed, and include principal plus interest paid on debts.

For most businesses (and for most bankers), income projections covering three years are more than adequate. In some cases, such as when you apply for a long-term loan, a longer projection may be requested. In general, though, the longer the projection, the less accurate it will be, and the less useful as a guide to action.

You don't need a crystal ball to make your projections. While no set of projections will be 100% accurate, experience and practice tend to make projections more precise. Even rough projections provide a set of benchmarks to measure your progress towards short-term goals. Like a sketchy map, rough projections are better than no directions at all.

If your projections are wildly incorrect, correct them. When to do this is a matter of judgment. A rule of thumb is that if a projected revenue or expense item is more than 20% off for a quarter (three months), revise it. If it is less than 20% off, wait for another quarter. Do not change your projections more often than quarterly. In a short period, many trends are distorted or magnified. These distortions will usually even out over a longer period. Of course, if you find you have omitted a major expense item or discover a significant new source of revenue, make immediate corrections.

Like a sketchy map, rough projections are better than no directions at all.

Figure 3.1:
Computers and Projections

Microcomputers and financial projections are meant to go together. A microcomputer and a spreadsheet program such as Excel™, Jazz™ or Lotus 1-2-3™ take the drudgery out of setting up and then tinkering with the income, cash flow and other projected financial statements.

Your accountant or other financial advisors may have already set up a template that fills your business-forecasting needs. A template is a pre-established set of commands for a specific software program, one which has already tested the arithmetic to make sure that the finished product (the projection) accurately reflects your data and assumptions. If not, they may be able to help you use your own software.

Business school students will help you computerize your projections. This is a less expensive option than utilizing professional help, but on the other hand, students may not provide the same depth of detail that your accountant or consultant would give you.

A modeling program such as Plans 'n Totals™ provides an integrated approach to preparing financial projections and budgets. You enter the data in common-sense formats, and at the end of the data entry, you can print out a comprehensive set of financial projections and budgets.

All your computer program can do, however, is process information that you provide. If your assumptions are off, your projections will be, too.

What's the great advantage of these programs?

Without going through hundreds of calculations, each one of which admits the possibility of innocent arithmetic error:

1. You can revise projections instantly, remedying omissions or correcting erroneous assumptions.
2. You can test hypotheses about price, debt load, fixed costs, unit sales and so on.
3. You can create a series of projections based on different sets of assumptions.
4. You can use more sophisticated financial analyses than were possible for a small business before the computer. Ask your accountant or banker about using (among other tools) internal rates of return and discounted future cash flows, establishing economic ordering quantities, or using break-even analysis in making pricing decisions.
5. Budget deviation analysis is greatly simplified. You can set up a program to automatically flag any projected item which exceeds the deviation limits you establish, whether in percentages, absolute dollars, or both.

In short, you have access to the level of financial management (including cash flow control) that used to be the province of big business.

The reasoning behind income projection is that since most revenues and expenses maintain the same patterns from one year to the next, the future will be much like the past. For example, if your gross margin has historically been 30% of net sales, you can safely assume (barring strong evidence to the contrary) that it will continue to be 30% of net sales for the immediate future.

If you are starting a business, look for financial statements and income ratios for businesses similar to yours. The *Robert Morris Associates' Annual Statement Studies* and trade-association figures are two good sources of "common-sized" financial statements. (A "common-sized" statement expresses sales, expense and balance sheet items as a percentage of total sales to facilitate comparison of a number of businesses of different sizes.) Check with your accountant and banker for other sources of information.

You have to be thorough and systematic when you prepare your income projection. The expense that bleeds your business dry (makes it illiquid) is almost always one which was overlooked or seriously misjudged—and therefore unplanned for. There are some expenses which cannot be foreseen. The best way to protect your business against these is to document all of your assumptions and be conservative in your estimates. "Conservative" means to understate your anticipated revenues and overstate expenses.

It is far better to exceed a conservative estimate than to fall below optimistic projections. However, being too far under creates a special set of problems—such as not having sufficient capital to finance growth. Basing income projections on hopes or unjustified fears is hazardous to your business' health. Be realistic.

Income statements and projections are standardized to make comparison and analysis easier. They must be dated to indicate the period of time they cover, and they must also contain notes to explain any unusual items such as windfall profits, litigation expenses and judgments, changes in depreciation schedules, and other material information. Assumptions should always be footnoted—to help remind you of how the numbers were originally obtained or justified, to provide a boost up the learning curve when you review your projections, and to help improve future projections.

Every month, compare your actual income and expenses against your projected income statements. (See Chapter Five: Use the Cash Flow Budget and Deviation Analysis for details). You want to detect deviations as soon as possible so you can correct problems before they get out of hand, and seize opportunities while they are still fresh.

Suggested formats for income statements (and projections) are shown in Figure 3.2. You may want to modify the example by adding or deleting a few expense or revenue items to fit your particular operation, but do not change the basic format.

Remember: The purpose of financial statements and projections is to provide you with the maximum amount of useful information and guidance, not to dazzle a prospective lender or investor.

The expense that bleeds your business dry is almost always one which was overlooked or seriously misjudged—and therefore unplanned for.

Figure 3.2:
Income Statement Format

(1) **Net Sales:**
(2) less **Cost of Goods Sold:**
(3) equals **Gross Margin:**
(4) **Operating Expenses:**
    Salaries and Wages
    Payroll Taxes and Benefits
    Rent
    Utilities
    Maintenance
    Office Supplies
    Postage
    Automobile and Truck
    Insurance
    Legal and Accounting
    Depreciation
    Others:

    _____
    _____
    _____

(5) **Other Expenses:**
    Interest
(6) **Total Expenses:**
(7) **Profit (Loss) Pre-Tax:**
(8) **Taxes:**
(9) **Net Profit (Loss):**

Explanation of Sample:
(1) **Net Sales:** Gross sales less returns, allowances and discounts.
(2) **Cost of Goods Sold:** Includes cost of inventories.
(3) **Gross Margin:** (1) Net Sales minus (2) Cost of Goods Sold. Represents the gross profit on sales without taking indirect costs into account.
(4) **Operating Expenses:** These are the costs which, together with (5) Other Expenses, must be met no matter what the sales level may be. The order in which they are stated isn't important. Thoroughness is. If some costs are trivial, lump them together under a heading of "miscellaneous," but be prepared to break them out if the miscellaneous totals more than an arbitrary 1% of Net Sales.
(5) **Other Expenses:** These are non-operating expenses. The most common is interest expense. It is helpful to display your interest expense in some detail to both highlight the cost of money and to provide easy access to information used for ratio analysis.
(6) **Total Expenses:** Sum of (4) Operating Expenses and (5) Other Expenses.
(7) **Profit (Loss) Pre-Tax:** (3) Gross Margin minus (6) Total Expenses. This is the tax base, the figure on which your tax will be calculated.
(8) **Taxes:** Consult your accountant.
(9) **Net Profit (Loss):** (7) minus (8). This represents the success or lack thereof for your business. There are three ways to make this figure more positive: increase gross margin, decrease total expenses, or both.

For the most useful projection, state your assumptions clearly. Do not put down numbers that you cannot rationally substantiate. Do not puff your gross sales projection to make the net profit positive. Give yourself conservative sales figures and pessimistic expense figures to make the success of your deal more probable. Be realistic.

You want your projections to reflect the realities of your business.

To prepare your income projections, use the data from Chapter Two. This proceeds logically. Enter the data on a 13-column spreadsheet which is set up according to the formats of Figures 3.3 (by month for the first year), 3.4 (by quarter for years two and three) and 3.5 (three-year summary).

You want your projections to reflect the realities of your business. They are models of your business (as are the cash flow projections in the next chapter), and should "look" like your business. To achieve this:

1. Take the gross sales and expense figures from your forecasts for the first year. Spread these across Figure 3.3, month by month.

   A. Start by spreading sales. Most businesses have a steady sales pattern that is peculiar to their business. Hospitality businesses in the northeast have one pattern; hospitality businesses in the southwest quite another. Some businesses concentrate 75% of their sales in the fourth quarter; others are steady throughout the year. You have to know your business cycle—and it must be reflected in your projections. When do you make the sales? Which are the fat months, and which are the lean ones?

   B. Some expenses are used evenly throughout the year. Legal and accounting, salaries, rent, utilities, etc., don't fluctuate much month to month. Take these evenly distributed expenses and divide by 12 to arrive at monthly figures.

   C. Some expenses are seasonal. You may have to hire extra help for Christmas, or to meet other seasonal demands. Take the amount in the forecast and spread it according to your estimate of when the expense will be incurred.

   D. Some expenses can be precisely timed. Acquiring equipment, incurring new debt, or paying off an old loan are examples. Build these into your projections. If you won't begin paying a higher rent until June, don't budget that rent in January. Use your common sense.

   E. Some expenses go up and down with sales. To spread these, you have to first spread your revenues, as you did above. Cost of Goods Sold, for example, is figured on sales. So are credit and collection costs. Check all of your variable expenses.

2. Once you have entered the figures for each month, calculate the Gross Margin, Operating Expense, Other Expense, Total Expense, and Profit (Loss) figures for each month. Cross-total to arrive at the yearly figures which will be used in Figure 3.5: Three-Year Summary.

3. Take the year-two and year-three forecasts and spread them by quarters. Allocate revenues and expenses to the quarters they appear in. The evenly-incurred expenses and so forth are treated just as they are for the monthly

projection, except that instead of dividing annual expense totals by 12 you divide the totals by 4. Enter the numbers on Figure 3.4.

4. The three-year summary is compiled from these first sets of projections. Take the yearly totals for years one, two and three and enter them on Figure 3.5.

Figure 3.3:
Income (Profit and Loss) Projection by Month

Set up this format on 13-column paper.

	Jan.	Feb.	Mar.	Apr.	May	...	Dec.
Sales							
Wholesale							
Retail							
Total Sales:							
Cost of Materials							
Variable Labor							
Cost of Goods Sold							
Gross Margin							
Operating Expenses							
Utilities							
Salaries							
Payroll Tax and							
Benefits							
Advertising							
Office Supplies							
Insurance							
Maintenance and							
Cleaning							
Legal and							
Accounting							
Delivery							
License Fees							
Telephones							
Depreciation							
Rent							
Miscellaneous							
Other Expenses							
Total Operating Expenses:							
Other Expenses:							
Interest (mortage)							
Interest (term loan)							
Interest (credit line)							
Others							
Total Other Expenses:							
Total Expenses:							
Net Profit (Loss) Pre-Tax:							

Figure 3.4:
**Income (Profit and Loss) Projection by Quarters
for Years Two and Three**

Set up this format on 13-column paper.

| | Year Two | | | | | Year Three | | | | |
| | Quarter | | | | | Quarter | | | | |
	1	2	3	4	Total	1	2	3	4	Total
Sales										
Wholesale										
Retail										
Total Sales:										
Cost of Materials										
Variable Labor										
Cost of Goods Sold										
Gross Margin										
Operating Expenses										
Utilities										
Salaries										
Payroll Tax and Benefits										
Advertising										
Office Supplies										
Insurance										
Maintenance and Cleaning										
Legal and Accounting										
Delivery										
License Fees										
Telephones										
Depreciation										
Rent										
Miscellaneous										
Other Expenses										
Total Operating Expenses:										
Other Expenses:										
Interest (mortage)										
Interest (term loan)										
Interest (credit line)										
Others										
Total Other Expenses:										
Total Expenses:										
Net Profit (Loss) Pre-Tax:										

Figure 3.5:
Income (Profit and Loss) Projection: Three-Year Summary

Set up this format on 13-column paper.

	Year 1	**Year 2**	**Year 3**
Sales			
Wholesale			
Retail			
Total Sales:			
Cost of Materials			
Variable Labor			
Cost of Goods Sold			
Gross Margin			
Operating Expenses			
Utilities			
Salaries			
Payroll Tax and			
Benefits			
Advertising			
Office Supplies			
Insurance			
Maintenance and			
Cleaning			
Legal and			
Accounting			
Delivery			
License Fees			
Telephones			
Depreciation			
Rent			
Miscellaneous			
Other Expenses			
Total Operating Expenses:			
Other Expenses:			
Interest (mortage)			
Interest (term loan)			
Interest (credit line)			
Others			
Total Other Expenses:			
Total Expenses:			
Net Profit (Loss) Pre-Tax:			

Once more, note that these projections lend themselves to modeling on a computerized spreadsheet. Check with your banker, accountant or other financial advisors—the chances of a minor arithmetic error blasting your budget's rationale is great, especially when you will be trying out different combinations of sales and expense figures to test your ideas.

Chapter Four:
Prepare Cash Flow Projections

If you were to be limited to one financial statement, the cash flow projection would be the one to pick. For a new or growing business it can make the difference between success and failure. For an ongoing business, it can make the difference between growth and stagnation.

Your cash flow projection is your most important cash flow control tool because:
1. It is your cash flow budget.
2. It pinpoints your financing needs.
3. It tells you whether and when to seek equity, debt, operating improvement or advice, or to sell off assets.

"Cash flow" is a highly descriptive term. Cash—liquid assets—flows into your business from a limited number of sources. It flows out through a much larger number of costs. Think of it as the lifeblood of your business. You can literally bleed a business—by taking too much cash out at the wrong time, or allowing many small costs to dribble cash away. You can give a business a transfusion: new capital or increased debt. Your job as the owner or manager is to make sure that you protect the cash flow, because positive cash flow (more coming in than going out) is survival, while negative cash flow (more going out than coming in) will sooner or later kill your business.

The cash flow projection (abbreviated to "cash flow") is more time sensitive than the income projection. It treats all and only cash items. For example, if you pay your insurance bill in four equal installments, you will have four disbursements (check written, sent, and cashed) on your cash flow, while on the income projection 12 equal expenses will be shown. The income projection has non-cash expenses such as depreciation and amortization. The cash flow doesn't touch these—but does show principal repayments on debt, which is not an expense item on the income statement. Keep in mind that the cash flow shows the movement of cash in and out of your business, while the income projection shows expenses and revenues as incurred, whether or not cash changes hands. Figure 4.1: Cash Flow Management Sketch provides a picture of cash flow.

The Cash Flow Management Sketch shows how cash flows in and out of the business over a stated period of time. Cash flows in from cash sales, collection of receivables, capital injections, etc., and flows out only through cash payments.

Your cash flow highlights the points in the calendar when the cash actually moves. The advantage of knowing ahead of time when more cash is needed is the ability to plan ahead for those outlays and not be forced into hasty, unexpected borrowing to meet cash needs.

Cash flow is the lifeblood of your business.

Lack of profits won't kill a business immediately. Although in the long run you have to make a profit to keep going, in the short run non-cash expenditures (depreciation, for example) can make your business show a loss, while the cash flow remains positive. Lack of cash to meet trade and other payables will kill your business quickly, unless new cash is found.

You can foresee the effect of new debt far more clearly in the cash flow than in the income projection. You may be able to find other ways to finance your business operations or minimize your credit needs given enough notice. Much of the advantage of studying your cash flow projection stems from timing: More options are available to you, at lower costs, with less panic.

Cash is primarily generated by sales. Perhaps your business is all cash—but if you offer any credit (charge accounts, term payments, trade credit) to your customers, you have to have a means of telling when those sales will turn into cash-in-hand. The impact of credit policy is blurred in the income projection, but made very clear in the cash flow projection. (See Chapter Six: Control Receivables and Inventory for more detail on credit and collection management.)

If your business is seasonal, the cash flow projection is vital. Liquidity planning is based on the cash flow—for example, in the garment trade, huge inventories are built up against a short, intense selling period. Timing in cash flow control is everything.

Preparing Your Cash Flow Projections

Prepare cash flow projections monthly for at least the next year, or until cash flow turns positive for three consecutive months. Quarterly figures will suffice for years two and three. A three-year summary is sometimes presented in a financing proposal, and serves as a helpful guideline in your business planning.

Cash flow projections lend themselves to computerization. Graphic displays make spreadsheet programs even more valuable, turning your numbers into more easily understood charts and graphs. You can make changes with much greater speed and accuracy than was possible with a sheaf of sharp #2 pencils, 13-column accounting paper and a well-worn eraser.

Use the cash flow management sketch (Figure 4.1) to help make sure you don't omit any cash flow item. Add any that are peculiar to your business. All of your disbursements must be recorded on your cash flow—all cash expenses, debt retirement, owner's withdrawals, capital purchases, everything that sucks away cash. Be thorough. Your checkbook can help remind you of amounts and timing. So can your cash journal (if you have one).

If you plan to expand your business or acquire or replace equipment, enter those costs and their timing. This gives you another chance to review your needs. You may want to apply the same best case/worst case/most likely case approach to acquisitions. Small-business owners have been known to make major purchases without adequate consideration of alternatives. If you have to disburse cash, make sure it goes for a legitimate business purpose.

text continued on page 20

Figure 4.1:
Cash Flow Management Sketch

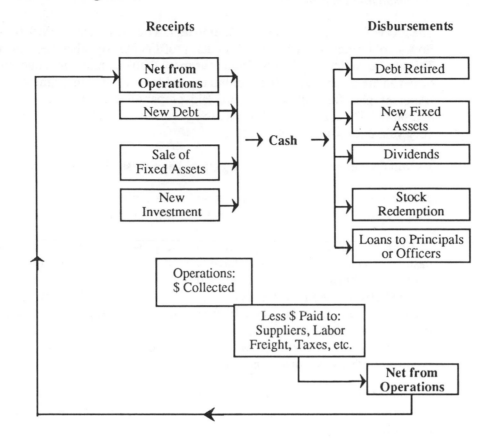

Receipts   **Disbursements**

Cash Flow Sketch

1. **Cash at Beginning of Period**
   Add Revenues, etc.:
2. Sales of products (cash)
3. Sales of products (receivables collected)
4. Cash received from assets sold
5. Cash received from equity investment
6. Cash received from loans
7. Cash received from bad debt recovery
8. Miscellaneous cash received
   Total: Cash Received

   Subtract: Cash Disbursements
9. New inventory purchased for cash
10. Salaries/wages
11. FICA, federal and state withholding tax
12. Fringe benefits paid
13. New equipment to be purchased for cash
    14. Processing equipment
    15. Office, sales equipment
    16. Transportation equipment
17. Insurance premiums
18. Fees
    19. Accounting
    20. Legal

21. Utilities
    22. Telephone
    23. Heat, light, power
24. Advertising
25. Principal and interest on debt
26. Transportation
    27. Oil, gas
    28. Vehicle maintenance
    29. Tires
30. Freight
31. Provision for bad debts (if funded with cash)
32. Taxes payable
    33. Income (state, federal, other if applicable)
    34. Property
    35. Excise
    36. Sales (if applicable)
37. Dividends paid, cash withdrawal by partner, or contribution to profit-sharing plan
38. Provision for unforeseen circumstances (if funded)
39. Provision for replacement of depreciable assets (if funded)

Total Cash Received Less Total Disbursements Equals Cash at End of Period

Note: Only cash disbursements are included. These are actual dollars that you pay out, not obligations that you incur now to be paid off at some future date. Those appear on the income projection and balance sheet.

Your cash flow projection is a working model of your business, and should reflect the actual patterns of cash use in the business.

text continued from page 18

The level of detail to provide is another matter. You may want to break the cash flow into a series of cash flows for each profit center or other business unit. This can be particularly handy if you have more than one major revenue stream, or if you are a manufacturer or contractor and have to prepare numerous bids. (Another plea for computerization: Bid preparation is streamlined by the computer.) The accumulated information gained by several projections can be a very valuable business asset.

As you prepare your cash flow projection, keep these eight points in mind:

1. Prepare the cash flow projection one line at a time, by month for the first year (Figure 4.2), and by quarters for years two and three (Figure 4.3).

2. Break the sales figures from your income projection into two categories: cash sales and credit sales. You have to plan on the credit sales turning into cash at a later date; how much later (and with what level of bad-debt loss) can be predicted on your past experience. Be conservative: If your customers usually pay in 15 days, count on the cash coming in 30 days later. If 30 days is the norm, count on a 45 day return. Cash sales are entered in the month of the sale. Cash receipts, however, will include credit sales from last month, not credit sales from the current month.

3. Cash receipts include cash flowing in from new investment, loans, bad-debt recovery, and miscellaneous sources including sale of fixed assets. Enter the amounts in the right months.

4. Some of your cash disbursements will be the same each month. (See Finest-kind's cash flow projection in Appendix One.) There is little virtue in entering the same figures in 12 monthly columns for Rent, Salaries, Benefits, and similar items that don't change. Lump them together (but provide a display so they can be broken out for closer scrutiny).

5. For all other items, put the disbursement in the month where the actual cash transaction occurs. If you pay legal and accounting fees quarterly, enter them in the month you pay the bill. If you buy supplies twice a year, when do you pay for them? If you plan to buy a piece of equipment, when do you have to pay for it—and where will the cash come from? Some bills get paid in greater or lesser amounts during the course of the year—utilities, advertising, and so on. Put down what you expect to pay in the appropriate months.

6. Once all the figures are entered on Figure 4.2, calculate Total Cash Received, Total Disbursements, and Cash Flow. A positive cash flow shows more coming in than going out. A negative cash flow is one where more goes out than comes in.

7. Use the same approach to handle the quarterly cash flow projections for years two and three in Figure 4.3. Your cash flow projection is a working model of your business, and should reflect the actual patterns of cash use in the business.

8. The Three-Year Summary (Figure 4.3) is derived from Figures 4.2 and 4.3.

Figure 4.2:
Cash Flow Projection by Month

Set up this format on 13-column paper.

	Jan.	Feb.	Mar.	...	Dec.	Total
Receipts						
Sales Receivable						
Wholesale						
Retail						
Other Services						
(see notes)						
Total Cash Receipts:						
Cash Disbursements						
Cost of Goods						
Variable Labor						
Advertising						
Insurance						
Legal and Accounting						
Delivery						
Fixed Cash Disbursements*						
Mortgage (rent)						
Term Loan						
Line of Credit						
Other (see notes)						
Total Cash Disbursements:						
Net Cash Flow:						
Cumulative Cash Flow:						
Cash on Hand						
Opening Balance						
+ Cash Received						
- Cash Disbursed						
New Balance:						
Total						
Fixed Cash Disbursements*/Year						
Fixed Cash Disbursements*/Month						

*Fixed Cash Disbursements
   Utilities
   Salaries
   Payroll Taxes and Benefits
   Office Supplies
   Maintenance and Cleaning
   License Fees
   Telephone
   Other

Figure 4.3
Cash Flow Projection by Quarter for Years Two and Three

Set up this format on 13-column paper.

| | Year Two Quarter | | | | | Year Three Quarter | | | | |
	1	2	3	4	Total	1	2	3	4	Total
Receipts										
Sales Receivable										
Wholesale										
Retail										
Other Services										
(see notes)										
Total Cash Receipts:										
Cash Disbursements										
Cost of Goods										
Variable Labor										
Advertising										
Insurance										
Legal and Accounting										
Delivery										
Fixed Cash Disbursements*										
Mortgage (rent)										
Term Loan										
Line of Credit										
Other (see notes)										
Total Cash Disbursements:										
Net Cash Flow:										
Cumulative Cash Flow:										
Cash on Hand										
Opening Balance										
+ Cash Received										
- Cash Disbursed										
New Balance:										
Total										
Fixed Cash Disbursements*/Year										
Fixed Cash Disbursements*/Month										
*Fixed Cash Disbursements										
Utilities										
Salaries										
Payroll Taxes and Benefits										
Office Supplies										
Maintenance and Cleaning										
License Fees										
Telephone										
Other										

Figure 4.4:
Cash Flow Projection: Three-Year Summary

Set up this format on 13-column paper.

	Year One	Year Two	Year Three
Receipts			
Sales Receivable			
Wholesale			
Retail			
Other Services			
(see notes)			
Total Cash Receipts:			
Cash Disbursements			
Cost of Goods			
Variable Labor			
Advertising			
Insurance			
Legal and Accounting			
Delivery			
Fixed Cash Disbursements*			
Mortgage (rent)			
Term Loan			
Line of Credit			
Other (see notes)			
Total Cash Disbursements:			
Net Cash Flow:			
Cumulative Cash Flow:			
Cash on Hand			
Opening Balance			
+ Cash Received			
- Cash Disbursed			
New Balance:			
Total			
Fixed Cash Disbursements*/Year			
Fixed Cash Disbursements*/Month			
*Fixed Cash Disbursements			
Utilities			
Salaries			
Payroll Taxes and Benefits			
Office Supplies			
Maintenance and Cleaning			
License Fees			
Telephone			
Other			

Chapter Five:
Use the Cash Flow Budget
and Deviation Analysis

Your cash flow and income projections are budgets which help keep your business heading towards your goals. Of the two, the cash flow budget is the most important. If you meet its forecasts, you will meet the profitability goals implicit in the income projection, and have cash left over to build the business with.

You create your budget under optimal conditions. All the information you have, with time to reflect upon it, improved by review and experience, gives you a sound budget. As mentioned earlier, anyone can set up a budget. The trick is to set up a budget worth following, and the step-by-step approach should have given this to you.

When you deviate from your budget, as you will, most likely you will do so under less than ideal conditions—panic, confusion, hustle and bustle, constant interruptions.

Decisions made under stress are seldom as fruitful as those made under calmer conditions. When a major change is forced upon you from outside, take notes. Keep a notebook to record your reasons, your response, and what happens—whether you made the right decision or not. This will help when you prepare the next version of your budget.

Do this faithfully. It pays off. You'll develop:
1. An excellent source of current information;
2. An accurate test of the projections you prepared; and
3. A fix on trends, both good and bad, that affect your business.

As you track actual versus projected performance, resist the urge to tinker too often with the budget. A budget is a guide that helps you maintain your business' focus. On the other hand, a budget shouldn't be a straitjacket. If you have sufficient reason to change your budgets, go ahead.

A budget is a guide that helps you maintain your business' focus.

Figure 5.1:
Creating Monthly Budgets

You may want to cast budgets (cash flow projections) every month, only one quarter at a time (yet another argument for a computerized spreadsheet approach). Each month, forecast and project for the next three months. This compresses your budgeting experience and vaults you up the learning curve. The monthly feedback on your old budgets guarantees better insight into the budgeting process.

By checking actual against budgeted figures each month, you will gain a heightened awareness of short-term trends, both in your business and in the general economy. For instance, personnel turnover will make a small business

Since you now know how much cash you need, when you need it, and for how long, you have the beginnings of a powerful financing proposal.

waver from its projections. As new personnel work into their jobs and become less demanding of more experienced personnel, productivity will rebound and the business will return to its projected course.

Review your achievements and budgets on a monthly basis, but don't change the budget unless your review suggests a major error in your projections. A budget is designed to assist in the normal operations of your business, not in unpredictable variations which are felt only for a week or a month. Keep a log of these extraordinary events, because seen from a longer view, they may form a subtle pattern to help you in the future.

What should you do if all cash outflows are justified and on time, yet planned cash inflow is inadequate? Then you have no choice. You have to generate additional cash somehow. With your cash flow budget at hand, this problem, while severe, is not insurmountable. You can establish a plan for positive cash flow based on facts, not terror.

1. Examine the cash flow disbursements one by one, looking for those items which can be rescheduled to ease your cash flow. Perhaps some payables can be renegotiated with your suppliers—they want you to stay in business. It's cheaper for them to help you over a rough spot than to develop a brand new customer. Insurance premiums might be stretched from quarterly to monthly, for example.

2. Make a list of the disbursements which cannot be changed to other dates. Salaries and taxes are on this list. Maybe you have to pare back operations, or reduce staff. While these may be last resorts, they should be considered.

3. List anticipated cash inflows, allowing a margin for safety. Maybe you can lean on your customers to pay in 30 instead of 45 days. Maybe you can get a large customer to prepay in exchange for a discount.

4. Go back to the items you can reschedule. Don't forget to take full advantage of trade credit, but don't abuse it. Maybe some of these disbursements can be postponed, or eliminated by tightening up and making do with other assets.

What happens if you still have shortfalls? Congratulate yourself for being realistic. The shortfall indicates a need for some kind of financing. Your cash flow gives you the amount, timing and duration of the financing need.

Since you now know how much cash you need, when you need it, and for how long, you have the beginnings of a powerful financing proposal.

Your well-documented cash flow budget is the heart of your financing proposal. It demonstrates that you know what you're doing and that you plan ahead and take all due precautions. Such careful management appeals to bankers.

Why? The cash flow budgeting process shows that you care enough about the future of your company to establish goals and the controls and routes to reach those goals. The implied discipline is impressive.

Deviation Analysis

Deviation analysis is a simple concept. You use your one-year and monthly cash flow and income projections as budgets, test actual against budgeted performance monthly, and flag any deviations from the budget. You will want to set some kinds of norms: a 20% deviation on any cash inflow or disbursement item would certainly call for your attention. Some managers flag any 5% deviation and exercise their judgment as to what to do with each one. Choose your own trigger points, in dollars or percentages.

The great advantage is that you will review monthly performance against the budget each month. You can identify opportunities and problems in time to turn them to your advantage.

The four Budget Deviation Forms are easy to use—feel free to copy them. Fill in the projected amounts, fill in the actual performance, and compare them.

Choose your own trigger points, in dollars or percentages.

27

Figure 5.2
Budget Deviation Analysis by Month

From the Income Statement

For the Month of _____

	A Actual for Month	B Budget for Month	C Deviation (B-A)	D % Deviation (C/B x 100)
Sales				
Less Cost of Goods				
Gross Profit on Sales				
Operating Expenses:				
Variable Expenses 　Sales Salaries (commissions) 　Advertising 　Miscellaneous Variable				
Total Variable Expenses				
Fixed Expenses 　Utilities 　Salaries 　Payroll Taxes and Benefits 　Office Supplies 　Insurance 　Maintenance and Cleaning 　Legal and Accounting 　Delivery 　Licenses 　Boxes, Paper, etc. 　Telephone 　Miscellaneous 　Depreciation 　Interest				
Total Fixed Expenses				
Total Operating Expenses				
Net Profit (Gross Profit on Sales less Total Operating Expenses)				
Tax Expense				
Net Profit After Taxes				

Figure 5.3
Budget Deviation Analysis Year-to-Date

From the Income Statement

Year-to-Date _____

	A **Actual for Year-to-Date**	B **Budget for Year-to-Date**	C **Deviation (B-A)**	D **% Deviation (C/B x 100)**
Sales				
Less Cost of Goods				
Gross Profit on Sales				
Operating Expenses:				
Variable Expenses Sales Salaries (commissions) Advertising Miscellaneous Variable				
Total Variable Expenses				
Fixed Expenses Utilities Salaries Payroll Taxes and Benefits Office Supplies Insurance Maintenance and Cleaning Legal and Accounting Delivery Licenses Boxes, Paper, etc. Telephone Miscellaneous Depreciation Interest				
Total Fixed Expenses				
Total Operating Expenses				
Net Profit (Gross Profit on Sales less Total Operating Expenses)				
Tax Expense				
Net Profit After Taxes				

Calculations: A. Add current month actual to last month's year-to-date analysis.
B. Add current month budget to last month's year-to-date analysis.

Figure 5.4
Budget Deviation Analysis by Month

From the Cash Flow

For the Month of _____

	A Actual for Month	B Budget for Month	C Deviation (B-A)	D % Deviation (C/B x 100)
Beginning Cash Balance				
Add:				
Cash Sales				
Accounts Receivable That Have Turned to Cash				
Other Cash Inflows				
Total Available Cash				
Deduct Estimated Disbursements:				
Cost of Materials Variable Labor Advertising Insurance Legal and Accounting Delivery Equipment* Loan Payments Mortgage Payment Property Tax Expense				
Deduct Fixed Cash Disbursements:				
Utilities Salaries Payroll Taxes and Benefits Office Supplies Maintenance and Cleaning Licenses Boxes, Paper, etc. Telephone Miscellaneous				
Total Disbursements				
Ending Cash Balance				

Equipment expense represents actual expenditures made for purchase of equipment.

Figure 5.5
Budget Deviation Analysis Year-to-Date

From the Cash Flow

Year-to-Date _____

	A Actual for Year-to-Date	B Budget for Year-to-Date	C Deviation (B-A)	D % Deviation (C/B x 100)
Beginning Cash Balance				
Add:				
Sales Revenue				
Other Revenue				
Total Available Cash				
Deduct Estimated Disbursements:				
Cost of Materials Variable Labor Advertising Insurance Legal and Accounting Delivery Equipment* Loan Payments Mortgage Payment Property Tax Expense				
Deduct Fixed Cash Disbursements:				
Utilities Salaries Payroll Taxes and Benefits Office Supplies Maintenance and Cleaning Licenses Boxes, Paper, etc. Telephone Miscellaneous				
Total Disbursements				
Ending Cash Balance				

Calculations: A. *Add current month actual to last month's year-to-date analysis.*

B. *Add current month budget to last month's year-to-date analysis.*

Equipment expense represents actual expenditures made for purchase of equipment.

Chapter Six:
Control Receivables and Inventory

Two of your largest current assets are receivables and inventory. In order to manage your cash flow, you want to turn these into cash as soon as possible. However, unless they are managed with cash flow in mind, they can become hidden cash drains.

The aim is profitability and positive cash flow, not sales increases.

To manage these assets properly, you must know:
1. The age of your receivables and inventory;
2. The turn of your receivables and inventory;
3. The concentration of your receivables (how many customers, what dollar amount of receivables they represent, what products the receivables cover); and
4. The concentration of your inventory by product lines.

You must also know what effect your credit and collection policies have on your working capital and cash flow. Small-business owners all too often mistake sales for profits. They extend more and more credit, practice lax collection policies, and end up providing interest-free loans to their customers in the name of "increasing sales." Many business owners have found that their largest accounts actually cost them money because of slow payment.

No small-business owner can afford to provide interest-free loans to his or her biggest customers, but unless you take the time to analyze the payment behavior of your slow-paying accounts, you may not know what's eating up your cash flow.

This isn't to say "Don't increase credit sales." The aim is profitability and positive cash flow, not sales increases. If the sales don't translate into bottom-line profits, then you are buying trouble as fast as you are buying sales.

Receivables Management

Begin by examining the age of your receivables every week. This helps you spot the slow-paying accounts early—so you can begin collection efforts as soon as possible.

Separate invoices into current, 30-days-old, 60-days, 90-days and over. This is called "aging the receivables": You want to set up your aging schedule on the credit terms you offer—current, 10-day, and so on. The main idea is to spot those customers who pay within term (so you can find more of them) and those who don't (so you can reeducate or avoid them in the future).

Then, figure out your collection period: Divide annual credit sales (from your historical figures or from projections) by 360 to find the average daily credit sale. Next, divide your current outstanding receivables total by the average daily credit sale figure. This gives you your current receivables collection period.

Don't forget to consider seasonality. If sales tend to cluster, your accounts receivable will peak at the time of sales and distort the collection picture. Department stores, for example, have huge receivables at the beginning of the year, much smaller receivables in the late spring.

A rule of thumb: If your collection period is more than one-third greater than your credit terms (for example, 40 days if your terms are net-30), you have a cash cycle or collection problem that needs your immediate attention.

Follow these five steps in receivables management:
1. *Age your receivables.*
2. *Calculate your collection period.* Use the rule of thumb to check for problems.
3. *Identify and vigorously pursue the slow-paying customers.*
4. *Identify and try to find more fast-paying or term-paying accounts.*
5. *Measure the impact of your credit and collection policies on your cash flow by playing "what-if" with your projections.*
Perhaps changing your terms could improve cash flow and profits.

Here is the formula to determine the length of your collection period: These figures come from Finestkind's income projection in Appendix One on page 53.

Yearly sales:
Wholesale	$ 90,000
Retail	126,000
Total sales:	$216,000

The first number to determine is the average daily credit sale. This is reached by dividing total annual credit sales by 360. In Finestkind's case, the retail sales are same-day cash sales. Of the wholesale accounts, let's assume that $43,200, or 20% of total sales, are on credit:

The average daily credit sale is: $43,200/360 = $120

Once the average daily credit sale is determined, divide it into the current outstanding receivables to find the collection period. Assume that Finestkind's accounts receivable figure is $5,000: $5,000/$120 = 41.6 days.

The result is that Finestkind is maintaining a 41.6-day collection period. This doesn't look bad—if their terms were net-30. Unhappily, their terms are net-10, so this is well beyond acceptable limits. The higher this collection period climbs, the more Finestkind will find itself getting out of the seafood business and into the banking business. Finestkind's management knows more about fish than financing, and should capitalize on that knowledge.

Credit and Collection

The cost of extending credit is a good example of the hidden costs that devour working capital. Most small-business owners aren't credit experts. They grant credit because other businesses do, and often fail to understand what the impact on profits and cash flow will be. Few small businesses have explicit credit and collection policies, so they lose twice: granting the credit, and then having to collect funds later. If you establish credit and collection policies appropriate to your business, you will increase profits, improve the quality of your current assets, and speed up your cash flow. Check with your banker, accountant, or other qualified professional and get the help and interest you deserve.

The cost of extending credit is a good example of the hidden costs that devour working capital.

Investigate the use of credit cards. These cost little in return for the headaches they can save you. Consider the cost, in direct bad-debt losses as well as in time, effort, and attention that slow-paying accounts cost you. Then add the costs of capital tied up in receivables to the interest you pay to carry those receivables. Is it worth it? Probably not—but you can get a dollars and cents answer from your accountant.

Inventory Management

Carrying costs of inventory run as high as 30% of average inventory, a substantial drain on working capital. Add the costs of insurance, storage, spoilage, pilferage, handling and maintenance to the cost of inventory loans. It adds up fast.

It's hard to determine the right amounts of inventory to carry. The balance is between stockout and unnecessary expenses, compounded by supplier delivery and reorder times. Some of the factors that your inventory policies should reflect (in addition to the marketing and sales factors, which are dominant):

1. How often do you turn (sell) your inventory? How does that compare with other businesses in your industry?

You can calculate your inventory-turnover ratios by following these formulas:

Cost of Goods Sold/Average Inventory (in $) = Inventory Turnover
Number of Days in Period*/Inventory Turnover = Inventory Turnover Days
Cost of Goods Sold/RMA Average Turnover** = Ideal Inventory

*360 days=1 year, 180 days=6 months, 30 days=1 month
**Robert Morris Associates' figures for your industry can be provided by your banker.

2. What is your reorder time? The difference between a 10-day reorder time and a 210-day reorder is enormous, and will affect the level of reserve inventory you carry.

3. Who are your suppliers? Where are they located? Delivery times are important.

Your job is to run your business, not to become a financing expert.

4. What trade terms do your suppliers give you? Taking a 2% discount on terms of 2/10, net-30 is equivalent to earning a 72% annual yield. That's considerably more than the interest your bank charges—and has implications for your ordering and inventory policies.

For some businesses, a "reserve-for-purchases" policy helps keep the cost of inventory down. Check with your accountant, banker, or other qualified financial advisor.

Remember: Your job is to run your business, not to become a financing expert. The correlation between business success and use of outside financial advisors is too well-documented to ignore.

Chapter Seven:
Managing Positive Cash Flow

Positive cash flow—the increase of cash in your business over a period of time—can come from a number of sources. Not all of them are due to good management.

You could experience excellent cash flow while going broke:
1. Stop paying your bills. While this may look good from a cash flow viewpoint, it will put you out of business.
2. Forget to pay taxes. More than one business has learned that borrowing from Uncle Sam is foolish, expensive and illegal.
3. Get a substantial amount of cash from a credulous investor. He or she may not realize that your enterprise is failing.

And so on. Not all sources of positive cash flow are beneficial or long-term.

Positive cash flow can come from neutral sources:
1. You have just landed a major contract and the retainer was paid in advance.
2. Your business is seasonal, and this is the time of year when cash rolls in.
3. You accrue funds all year long to make a lump-sum payment into a pension plan and the bill is due next month.

And so on. Most of the time, positive cash flow results from a combination of these neutral sources, with some operating profits tossed in.

The ideal sources of positive cash flow are the ones we all strive for:
1. You really are making a lot of money.
2. Sales are up, costs are down.
3. Prior investments pay off.

Basically, positive cash flow comes from four sources:
1. New investment;
2. New debt;
3. Sale of assets, including sale/leasebacks; and
4. Operating profits.

The first three are limited, because if the fourth doesn't chip in regularly, you run out of investors, your creditors pull the plug, and you'll have no more assets to sell.

Hence the need to carefully ascertain where your positive cash flow is coming from.

·Once you've identified the sources, your strategies for using the excess cash can be formulated—but not before. For example, if the sources are a new contract, operating efficiencies due to investment in new equipment, and your ascent up the learning curve, plus a few deferred expenses, you might choose an aggressive strategy. However, if the sources are unpaid bills, unpaid taxes, and sale of your one money-making division, a far different strategy is in order.

Your strategy has to reflect your anticipated cash flows, too. You may find, for instance, that some of the idle cash can be salted away for future growth, while some has to be kept liquid to meet next month's anticipated cash shortfall.

How should you manage your surplus cash?

1. Establish priorities. Positive cash flow from operations creates opportunities to make more money.

Look at the rates of return of available options. Those items with the greatest potential impact on your bottom line are those which either increase revenues (without driving fixed costs out of sight) or decrease expenses. New equipment might further both goals. Reducing debt is always an option. So is increasing advertising and marketing.

The top priority is usually reduction of short-term debt. It is easier to deposit cash against a line of credit than to invest it wisely. Any money not needed for immediate requirements (bringing trade bills current, paying taxes, meeting the payroll) should be used to pay off short-term debt for two reasons:
    A. You will save substantial interest costs.
    B. Your banker will be more amenable to increasing your credit line if he or she can see periods when your line of credit was only partially extended.

2. Research investment strategies and opportunities. There are all too many ways to invest excess cash.

Some of the questions to ask yourself, once immediate priorities have been satisfied and short-term debt paid out, concern:
    A. Security. How safe is my money? Will it be there when I need it?
    B. Liquidity. While high-rate, long-term certificates of deposit have their uses, what happens if I need money next month, not two years from now?
    C. Yield. Before investing, would the money earn more if reinvested in my company than if it were put in a cash management account? Or would a short-term investment provide the right mix of yield and liquidity for my company at this time?

Keep your aims clear. You want safety and liquidity first, then yield. This doesn't mean to let excess cash sit idle—just that your business should be making its profits on operations, not investments.

3. Choose the appropriate strategy and stick to it. Based on your analysis of your business' cash flow and financing needs, you can begin to maximize returns on your excess cash. Be consistent, and be sure that your strategies are in line with your business plan.

For example, suppose that you decide the best strategy is to set up a bank sweep account to be activated whenever balances rise above a preset level. This allows current obligations to be funded, yet makes sure that your money works for you. Excess cash will be swept daily into a high-interest money market account, yet be immediately available if needed for operations. This option satisfies all three demands: safety, liquidity, and yield.

Summary

Controlling cash flow is not mysterious at all. The tools you use are accurate financial information and forecasts based on your experience and your company's historical performance.

If you don't have clear, accurate, timely financial information, you need a new accountant. Information—factual, detailed information—is needed to run your business.

Your cash flow management strategies depend on your business plan. What are your goals? What resources do you have available? What are your financial needs, personnel needs, marketing needs? All of these reflect different systems in your business. Each one influences the others, so in a very real sense it doesn't pay to devote all of your attention to one or a few. All need to be managed.

In other words, your cash flow strategy must be an extension of your business plan. Cash flow control involves more than money flowing in and out of your business. It involves every aspect of your entire business.

Factual, detailed information is needed to run your business.

Appendix One

Finestkind Seafoods' Financial Statements

The Balance Sheet for Finestkind Seafoods, Inc.

Balance sheets are designed to show how the assets, liabilities and net worth of a company are distributed at a given point in time. The format is standardized to facilitate analysis and comparison—do not deviate from it.

Balance sheets for all companies, great and small, contain the same categories arranged in the same order. The difference is one of detail. Your balance sheet should be designed with your business information needs in mind. These will differ according to the kind of business you are in, the size of your business, and the amount of information which your bookkeeping and accounting systems make available.

Balance sheets for all companies contain the same categories arranged in the same order.

Sample Balance Sheet Format

Name of Business
Date (month, day, year)
Balance Sheet

Assets

Current Assets		$ _____
Fixed Assets	$ _____	
Less Accumulated Depreciation	$ _____	
Net Fixed Assets		$ _____
Other Assets		$ _____
Total Assets:		$ _____

Footnotes

Liabilities

Current Liabilities	$ _____
Long-Term Liabilities	$ _____
Total Liabilities:	$ _____

Net Worth (total assets minus total liabilities) or

Owner's Equity	$ _____
Total Liabilities and Net Worth	$ _____

Footnotes

The categories can be defined more precisely. However, the order of the categories is important and you should follow it. They are arranged in order of decreasing liquidity (for assets) and decreasing immediacy (for liabilities).

A brief description of each principal category follows:

1. Current Assets: cash, government securities, marketable securities, notes receivable (other than from officers or employees), accounts receivable, inventories, prepaid expenses, any other item which will or could be converted to cash in the normal course of business within one year.

2. Fixed Assets: land, plant, equipment, leasehold improvements, other items which have an expected useful business life measured in years. Depreciation is applied to those fixed assets which (unlike land) will wear out. The fixed asset value of a depreciable item is shown as the net of cost minus accumulated depreciation.

3. Other Assets: intangible assets such as patents, copyrights, exclusive use contracts, notes receivable from officers and employees.

4. Current Liabilities: accounts payable, notes payable, accrued expenses (wages, salaries, withholding tax, FICA), taxes payable, current portion of long-term debt, other obligations coming due within one year.

5. Long-Term Liabilities: mortgages, trust deeds, intermediate and long-term bank loans, equipment loans (all of these net of the current portion of long-term debt, which appears as a current liability).

6. Net Worth: owner's equity, retained earnings, other equity.

7. Footnotes: You should provide displays of any extraordinary item (for example, a schedule of payables). Contingent liabilities such as pending lawsuits should be included in the footnotes. Changes of accounting practices would also be mentioned here.

If you need to provide more detail, do so—but remember to follow the standard format. If your balance sheet is assembled by an accountant, the accountant will specify whether it is done with or without audit. If you do it yourself, it is without audit. The decision to use a CPA (Certified Public Accountant) should be made carefully for tax and other legal reasons.

A sample balance sheet for Finestkind follows on the next page.

Finestkind Seafoods, Inc.
October 1, 19—

Balance Sheet

Assets

Current Assets:

Cash	$ 2,150
Accounts Receivable (net)	1,700
Merchandise Inventory	3,900
Supplies	450
Pre-Paid Expenses	320
Total Current Assets:	**$ 8,520**

Fixed Assets:

Fixtures and Leasehold Improvements (d)	$13,265
Building (freezer)	4,500
Equipment	3,115
Trucks	6,500
Total Fixed Assets:	**$27,380**
Total Assets:	**$35,900**

Liabilities

Current Liabilities:

Accounts Payable	$ 8,077
Current Portion Long-Term Debt	1,440
Total Current Liabilities:	**$ 9,517**

Long-Term Liabilities:

Note Payable (a)	$ 535
Bank Loan Payable (b)	1,360
Equity Loan Payable (c)	9,250
Total Long-Term Liabilities:	**$11,145**
Total Liabilities:	**$20,662**

Net Worth:

Owners' Equity	$15,238
Total Liabilities and Net Worth:	**$35,900**

Accounts payable display:		
	Eldredge's Inc.	$3,700
	Lesswing's	4,119
	Paxstone	180
	B&B Refrigeration	78
		$8,077

(a) Dave N. Hall for electrical work.
(b) Term loan secured by 1974 Jeep, 1983 Ford.
(c) S & C Finance Corp., Anytown, ME
(d) Includes $10,000 in improvements since June. See appraisal in Supporting Document section.

The balance sheet for Finestkind provides a level of detail appropriate for the purposes of the principals, who own all of the stock.

The balance sheet for Finestkind is modestly detailed. No depreciation has been taken, for example, because the business has just been started. The Net Worth section could have been more complex. The important thing to notice is that it provides a level of detail appropriate for the purposes of the principals, who own all of the stock.

Some financing sources (banks or other investors) may want to see balance sheets projected for each quarter for the first year of operation and annually for the next two. This would quickly show changes in debt, net worth, and the general condition of the business, and could be another helpful control document. You may wish to have a monthly balance sheet (easily done with a micro-computer-powered accounting system), but for many businesses, a year-end balance sheet is all that is required.

Income Projections for Finestkind Seafoods, Inc.

Explanation for Income Statement Projections

This section will:
- A. Explain how the figures on the projection were calculated.
- B. Detail the assumptions which were made. Numerical references have been made by line—for example, (21) Maintenance and Cleaning.

The degree of pessimism you should build into a projection is a matter of judgment.

(3) **Sales** include sales of seafood and ancillary products such as seasonings, sauces, baitbags, bait. In the future, some tourist items may be included.

(4) **Wholesale** and (5) **Retail**. Finestkind plans to service the wholesale trade more extensively than is shown here, although the trend has been built into the calculations. Due to a major marketing effort [see (18) **Advertising** below], wholesale sales should increase to 60% of gross sales within two years. Retail sales are expected to be more volatile than the wholesale business, leveling off around $20,000/month due to space restrictions. Volatility is seasonal, building from late March to a late summer peak. The increases shown in (4) **Wholesale** are based both on the greater number of restaurants open in the summer and the intense marketing efforts, planned for the winter months, to sell directly to the many restaurants which don't yet know Finestkind. Wholesale sales for September of the preceding year were $9,600, so these figures are perhaps more conservative than they need to be.

(4) **Wholesale** in Years Two and Three follow the same pattern as Year One (seasonality) but start at $10,000/October Year Two as the result of advertising and marketing efforts, longer experience with the wholesale market, and greater exposure to the market. Year Three is a bit more seasonal, reflecting a flattening out of the sales curve.

The degree of pessimism you should build into a projection is a matter of judgment. Some is good; too much can be bad, as it will distort a reasonably good game plan and make a realistic deal look too risky.

(6) **Total Sales.** (4) plus (5).

(8) **Cost of Materials.** Finestkind's inventory has an average cost of 68% of sales (including a start-up spoilage rate of 5% which has been reduced to under 1% of sales), and has been calculated as 72% of sales to allow for the fluctuation of dockside prices during the winter.

(9) **Variable Labor.** In Years One and Two, two part-time summer helpers will be needed: a counter person at $4/hour for 16 hours/week for 10 weeks, and a fish cutter at $6.75/hour for 20 hours/week for 16 weeks. In Year Three, two full-time counter helpers and a full-time cutter will be needed for 10 and 16 weeks, respectively.

(10) Cost of Goods Sold. (8) plus (9).

(12) Gross Margin. (6) minus (10).

(14) Operating Expenses. These are (by and large) the fixed expenses, those which don't vary directly with sales levels. Keeping control of operating expenses is immensely important and easily overlooked, perhaps because so much emphasis is placed on generating sales. A profitable business needs to control costs and maintain (or increase) sales.

(15) Utilities. Prorated by agreement with the utility companies. Goes from $165/month (Year One) to $220 to $240 in Year Three. It will probably change as new equipment and better insulation are installed.

(16) Salaries.

Year One:	$950/month for Gosling and Swan
Year Two:	$1,200/month for Gosling and Swan
	$850/month for a full-time employee
Year Three:	$1,500/month for Gosling and Swan
	$900/month ($50/month raise) for employee

Salaries are lower than Finestkind would pay for a professional manager in order to preserve scarce capital (they are undercapitalized, and the salaries reflect "sweat equity"). As the business grows, they hope to take annual bonuses based on profits—after capital needs are met.

(17) Payroll Taxes and Benefits. 12.5% of (16). This is low; in many businesses fringe benefits alone are over 25% of salaries. In a small business, benefits are more often than not skimpy.

(18) Advertising. Local newspaper and radio spots. This is an expense that Finestkind might profitably increase. They reason (correctly) that a consistent, though modest, campaign will be more productive than sporadic, intensive promotions. The advertising budget is 2.5% of (6) Total Sales. In Year One, a large one-time promotional blitz will be made in April to build off-season wholesale business.

(20) Insurance. Includes liability, workers compensation, vehicle and other normal forms of insurance. As the business can afford it, they will add key-man disability to the life insurance coverage. Year Two reflects the increase in workers comp and the property insurances.

(21) Maintenance and Cleaning. Mainly supplies—a food market must meet stringent health codes.

(22) Legal and Accounting. Retainers to attorney and accountant, used to smooth out cash flow. Otherwise occasional large bills would distort monthly income projection figures, even though the use of these services is spread evenly over the year.

(23) Delivery Expenses. Delivery of merchandise to restaurants and other markets. Year Two: 2% of total sales; Year Three: 1.7%. As the wholesale business increases, route efficiency should also increase, causing delivery expenses as a percentage of sales to decrease.

(24) Licenses. Required by state and local authorities.

(25) Boxes, Paper, etc. Packaging supplies, which are a semi-fixed expense.

(26) Telephone. Needed for sales, pricing, contacting suppliers and markets.

(27) Depreciation. Five-year, straight-line on equipment (beginning April, Year One); straight-line 19 years on building (beginning January, Year One). These are based on the assumption that 1/5 and 1/19 respectively will be "used up" in the normal course of doing business. Some businesses try to set this sum aside as a replacement fund.

(28) Miscellaneous. Operating expenses too small to be itemized.

(29) Rent. Applicable for three months in Year One; will be replaced by (33) Mortgage Interest on the income statement. The principal payments show up on the cash flow projections as part of mortgage payments. (The $876/month includes both principal and interest. Principal payments on loans do not appear as income statement items.)

(30) Total Operating Expenses. Sum of (15) through (29).

(32) Other Expenses. Non-operating costs are broken out to give them special prominence.

(33) Interest (Mortgage). $75,000 mortgage for 15 years at 11.5%. This is a normal term and interest rate for commercial buildings at this time. More than 15 years is rare.

(34) Interest (Term Loan). $30,000 loan for seven years at 12.25%. A rule of thumb: The longer the term, the higher the risk to the bank—so the higher the interest rate to you.

(35) Interest (Credit Line). Estimated use of line: average of $7,500 outstanding for six months a year at 13.5%. Lines of credit are not intended to replace permanent capital or long-term credit needs.

(36) Total Other Expenses. Sum of (33), (34), (35).

(37) Total Expenses. Sum of (30) and (36).

(39) Net Profit (Loss) Pre-Tax. (12) Gross Margin minus (37) Total Expenses. On this statement (and the other projections) a tax liability should be imputed. We left that liability off as it will vary from one state to another and with the legal structure of your business. Make sure to check with your accountant to arrive at a true net profit (loss) figure. As one banker puts it, "There is no such thing as a pre-tax profit."

As one banker puts it, "There is no such thing as a pre-tax profit."

Information is the most valuable result of financial statements.

Finestkind does not expect to make much money for the first few years. This is no surprise for a business so thinly capitalized. Even if there were no debt at all, net profit would have been only $8,000 for the year, or less than 4% of sales.

This is a projection based on conservative figures. In their more optimistic moments, Gosling and Swan hope to hold fixed costs to $4,500/month, not the $5,200 projected, and increase sales 12.5%. Their budgeted net profit would be around $18,000, not the projected loss of $5,710. If their gross margin were to continue at 30% of sales, not the 28% projected, their net profit would be over $18,000, their "best-case" assumption.

One item which should be mentioned again is rent. The cost of space appears on the cash flow as mortgage ($876/month). Another is loan amortization, which also appears on the cash flow as term loan ($534/month). These include interest and debt retirement, which are not expenses since they are for capital improvements that will be written off as "depreciation expense" over the course of several years. It is important not to double-deduct expenses: Such a practice is not only illegal but also obscures the information about your business.

Information is the most valuable result of financial statements. Accurate, timely information helps you run your business.

Income Projection by Month, Year One

	October	November	December	January 19--	February	March	April	May	June	July	August	September	Total
Sales													
Wholesale	$4,000	$4,000	$5,200	$5,600	$6,000	$7,000	$7,000	$8,400	$10,600	$11,300	$11,300	$9,600	$90,000
Retail	$9,730	$9,500	$9,500	$9,000	$8,400	$8,750	$10,300	$11,540	$12,165	$12,165	$12,475	$12,475	$126,000
Total Sales:	$13,730	$13,500	$14,700	$14,600	$14,400	$15,750	$17,300	$19,940	$22,765	$23,465	$23,775	$22,075	$216,000
Cost of Materials	$9,885	$9,720	$10,584	$10,512	$10,368	$11,340	$12,456	$14,357	$16,391	$16,895	$17,118	$15,894	$155,520
Variable Labor									$604	$796	$796	$604	$2,800
Cost of Goods Sold	$9,885	$9,720	$10,584	$10,512	$10,368	$11,340	$12,456	$14,357	$16,995	$17,691	$17,914	$16,498	$158,320
Gross Margin	$3,845	$3,780	$4,116	$4,088	$4,032	$4,410	$4,844	$5,583	$5,770	$5,774	$5,861	$5,577	$57,680
Operating Expenses													
Utilities	$160	$165	$180	$200	$200	$180	$170	$165	$185	$185	$185	$185	$2,160
Salaries	$1,900	$1,900	$1,900	$1,900	$1,900	$1,900	$1,900	$1,900	$1,900	$1,900	$1,900	$1,900	$22,800
Payroll Taxes and Benefits	$237	$238	$237	$238	$237	$238	$237	$238	$237	$238	$237	$238	$2,850
Advertising	$450	$450	$450	$450	$450	$450	$4,605	$450	$450	$450	$450	$450	$9,555
Office Supplies	$25	$25	$25	$25	$25	$25	$25	$25	$25	$25	$25	$25	$300
Insurance	$70	$70	$70	$110	$110	$110	$110	$110	$110	$110	$110	$110	$1,200
Maintenance and Cleaning	$25	$25	$25	$25	$25	$25	$25	$25	$25	$25	$25	$25	$300
Legal and Accounting	$125	$125	$125	$125	$125	$125	$125	$125	$125	$125	$125	$125	$1,500
Delivery Expenses	$150	$150	$150	$150	$150	$150	$150	$150	$150	$150	$150	$150	$1,800
Licenses	$9	$9	$9	$9	$9	$10	$10	$10	$10	$10	$10	$10	$115
Boxes, Paper, etc.	$15	$15	$15	$15	$20	$35	$40	$45	$50	$50	$50	$50	$400
Telephone	$85	$85	$85	$85	$85	$85	$85	$85	$85	$85	$85	$85	$1,020
Depreciation	$0	$0	$0	$455	$460	$460	$1,050	$1,055	$1,055	$1,055	$1,055	$1,055	$7,700
Miscellaneous													$0
Rent	$550	$550	$550	$0	$0	$0	$0	$0	$0	$0	$0	$1,650	$3,300
Total Operating Expenses:	$3,801	$3,807	$3,821	$3,787	$3,796	$3,793	$8,532	$4,383	$4,407	$4,408	$4,407	$6,058	$55,000
Other Expenses													
Interest (Mortgage)	$0	$0	$0	$695	$695	$696	$695	$695	$696	$695	$695	$696	$6,258
Interest (Term Loan)	$0	$0	$0	$0	$0	$0	$272	$272	$272	$272	$272	$272	$1,632
Interest (Credit Line)	$0	$85	$85	$0	$0	$0	$0	$0	$165	$165	$0	$0	$500
Total Other Expenses:	$0	$85	$85	$695	$695	$696	$967	$967	$1,133	$1,132	$967	$968	$8,390
Total Expenses:	$3,801	$3,892	$3,906	$4,482	$4,491	$4,489	$9,499	$5,350	$5,540	$5,540	$5,374	$7,026	$63,390
Net Profit (Loss) Pre-Tax:	$44	($112)	$210	($394)	($459)	($79)	($4,655)	$233	$230	$234	$487	($1,449)	($5,710)

Cumulative Loss: ($5,445) — Low Point (at April)

This spreadsheet was prepared using the Excel spreadsheet program from Microsoft.®

Income Projection by Quarter, Year Two

	A	B	C	D	E	F
		1st Quarter	2nd Quarter	3rd Quarter	4th Quareter	Total
1						
2						
3	Sales					
4	Wholesale	$38,900	$54,800	$76,500	$94,800	$265,000
5	Retail	$41,000	$37,400	$48,600	$53,000	$180,000
6	Total Sales:	$79,900	$92,200	$125,100	$147,800	$445,000
7						
8	Cost of Materials	$57,528	$66,384	$90,072	$106,416	$320,400
9	Variable Labor	$0	$0	$604	$2,196	$2,800
10	Cost of Goods Sold	$57,528	$66,384	$90,676	$108,612	$323,200
11						
12	Gross Margin	$22,372	$25,816	$34,424	$39,188	$121,800
13						
14	Operating Expenses					
15	Utilities	$660	$660	$660	$660	$2,640
16	Salaries	$9,750	$9,750	$9,750	$9,750	$39,000
17	Payroll Taxes and Benefits	$1,218	$1,218	$1,219	$1,220	$4,875
18	Advertising	$2,000	$2,305	$3,125	$3,695	$11,125
19	Office Supplies	$90	$90	$90	$90	$360
20	Insurance	$950	$950	$950	$950	$3,800
21	Maintenance and Cleaning	$90	$90	$90	$90	$360
22	Legal and Accounting	$500	$500	$500	$500	$2,000
23	Delivery Expenses	$1,598	$1,844	$2,502	$2,956	$8,900
24	Licenses	$25	$30	$30	$30	$115
25	Boxes, Paper, etc.	$150	$175	$225	$250	$800
26	Telephone	$450	$450	$450	$450	$1,800
27	Depreciation	$3,125	$3,125	$3,125	$3,125	$12,500
28	Miscellaneous	$150	$150	$150	$150	$600
29	Rent					
30	Total Operating Expenses:	$20,756	$21,337	$22,866	$23,916	$88,875
31						
32	Other Expenses					$0
33	Interest (Mortgage)	$2,070	$2,070	$2,070	$2,070	$8,280
34	Interest (Term Loan)	$798	$798	$797	$796	$3,189
35	Interest (Credit Line)			$140	$360	$500
35	Total Other Expenses:	$2,868	$2,868	$3,007	$3,226	$11,969
37	Total Expenses:	$23,624	$24,205	$25,873	$27,142	$100,844
38						
39	Net Profit (Loss) Pre-Tax:	($1,252)	$1,611	$8,551	$12,046	$20,956

This spreadsheet was prepared using the Excel spreadsheet program from Microsoft.®

Income Projection by Quarter, Year Three

	A	B	C	D	E	F
		1st Quarter	2nd Quarter	3rd Quarter	4th Quarter	Total
1		1st Quarter	2nd Quarter	3rd Quarter	4th Quarter	Total
2						
3	Sales					
4	Wholesale	$58,750	$55,000	$97,500	$113,750	$325,000
5	Retail	$47,400	$43,600	$56,000	$63,000	$210,000
6	Total Sales:	$106,150	$98,600	$153,500	$176,750	$535,000
7						
8	Cost of Materials	$76,428	$70,992	$110,520	$127,260	$385,200
9	Variable Labor	$0	$0	$1,622	$5,898	$7,520
10	Cost of Goods Sold	$76,428	$70,992	$112,142	$133,158	$392,720
11						
12	Gross Margin	$29,722	$27,608	$41,358	$43,592	$142,280
13						
14	Operating Expenses					
15	Utilities	$720	$720	$720	$720	$2,880
16	Salaries	$11,700	$11,700	$11,700	$11,700	$46,800
17	Payroll Taxes and Benefits	$1,462	$1,462	$1,463	$1,463	$5,850
18	Advertising	$2,655	$2,465	$3,835	$4,420	$13,375
19	Office Supplies	$120	$120	$120	$120	$480
20	Insurance	$1,025	$1,025	$1,025	$1,025	$4,100
21	Maintenance and Cleaning	$105	$105	$105	$105	$420
22	Legal and Accounting	$625	$625	$625	$625	$2,500
23	Delivery Expenses	$1,805	$1,675	$2,610	$3,010	$9,100
24	Licenses	$25	$30	$30	$30	$115
25	Boxes, Paper, etc.	$200	$200	$350	$450	$1,200
26	Telephone	$600	$600	$600	$600	$2,400
27	Depreciation	$3,125	$3,125	$3,125	$3,125	$12,500
28	Miscellaneous	$180	$180	$180	$180	$720
29	Rent					
30	Total Operating Expenses:	$24,347	$24,032	$26,488	$27,573	$102,440
31						
32	Other Expenses					
33	Interest (Mortgage)	$2,013	$2,013	$2,013	$2,013	$8,052
34	Interest (Term Loan)	$725	$725	$725	$725	$2,900
35	Interest (Line of Credit)			$140	$360	$500
36	Total Other Expenses:	$2,738	$2,738	$2,878	$3,098	$11,452
37	Total Expenses:	$27,085	$26,770	$29,366	$30,671	$113,892
38						
39	Net Profit (Loss) Pre-Tax:	$2,637	$838	$11,992	$12,921	$28,388

This spreadsheet was prepared using the Excel spreadsheet program from Microsoft.®

Income Projection: Three-Year Summary

	A	B	C	D
		Year 1	Year 2	Year 3
1		Year 1	Year 2	Year 3
2				
3	Sales			
4	Wholesale	$90,000	$265,000	$325,000
5	Retail	$126,000	$180,000	$210,000
6	Total Sales:	$216,000	$445,000	$535,000
7				
8	V* Cost of Materials	$155,520	$320,400	$385,200
9	V Variable Labor	$2,800	$2,800	$7,520
10	Cost of Goods Sold	$158,320	$323,200	$392,720
11				
12	Gross Margin	$57,680	$121,800	$142,280
13				
14	Operating Expenses			
15	F Utilities	$2,160	$2,640	$2,880
16	F Salaries	$22,800	$39,000	$46,800
17	V/F Payroll Taxes and Benefits	$2,850	$4,875	$5,850
18	F Advertising	$9,555	$11,125	$13,375
19	F Office Supplies	$300	$360	$480
20	F Insurance	$1,200	$3,800	$4,100
21	F Maintenance and Cleaning	$300	$360	$420
22	F Legal and Accounting	$1,500	$2,000	$2,500
23	V/F Delivery Expenses	$1,800	$8,900	$9,100
24	F Licenses	$115	$115	$115
25	V/F Boxes, Paper, etc.	$400	$800	$1,200
26	F Telephone	$1,020	$1,800	$2,400
27	F Depreciation	$7,700	$12,500	$12,500
28	F Miscellaneous	$0	$600	$720
29	F Rent	$3,300	$0	$0
30	Total Operating Expenses:	$55,000	$88,875	$102,440
31				
32	Other Expenses			
33	Interest (Mortgage)	$6,258	$8,280	$8,052
34	Interest (Term Loan)	$1,632	$3,189	$2,900
35	Interest (Line of Credit)	$500	$500	$500
36	Total Other Expenses:	$8,390	$11,969	$11,452
37	Total Expenses:	$63,390	$100,844	$113,892
38				
39	Net Profit (Loss) Pre-Tax	($5,710)	$20,956	$28,388
40				
41	*V=Variable Cost, F=Fixed Cost			

This spreadsheet was prepared using the Excel spreadsheet program from Microsoft.®

Cash Flow Projections for Finestkind Seafoods, Inc.

Explanation for Cash Flow Projections

The receipts shown on these cash flow projections include both sales and other cash sources to emphasize their impact on Finestkind. The cash flow projections show how business operations affect cash flow, so some people prefer to isolate "Other Sources" of cash receipts in the cash reconciliation section [lines (40)-(43) in the Year One Cash Flow Projection]. References are to line numbers on the accounting sheet unless otherwise noted.

(3) Sales Receivable. Sales are cash for retail, cash or 10-day net for wholesale accounts. If Finestkind provided longer terms, their cash flow could be significantly altered. As it is, the cash flow assumes a conservative 10-day lag on all wholesale sales. Since wholesale sales in September were $6,000, $2,000 (10/30 of September wholesale sales) turns to cash in October.

The same rationale applies to the rest of the year: One-third of wholesale receipts aren't collected until the following month.

The collection lag is not continued beyond the first quarter of Year Two. Experience will correct the cash flow, and new figures should be calculated for Year Two on a monthly basis for Year-Two business planning.

(4) Wholesale. Note the total of $28,700 + 60,100 (Total Sales Receivable and Total Wholesale) = $88,000, which is $1,200 less than the projected sales of $90,000 shown on the income statement. To reconcile the difference between these figures, note that $2,000 in cash receipts come from September of the preceding year, while $3,200 of cash receipts are postponed for September of Year One. Sales figures are based on the Income Projections on pages 53 to 56.

(5) Retail. See Income Projections on pages 53 to 56.

(6) Other Sources.

October:	Inventory loan using credit line
November:	Closing costs, using credit line
January:	Purchase building; $30,000 from Gosling and Swan as new equity investment, along with a $75,000 mortgage
April:	Equipment and building improvements, from term loan
June:	Inventory loan, credit line

(7) Total. Cash Receipts are the sum of (3) + (4) + (5) + (6). Note that the total is distorted by loans and new investment.

(8) Cash Disbursements. These are the disbursements which will be made in cash (including checks) during the normal course of business plus any major anticipated cash outlays.

(9) Cost of Goods. From Income Projection on page 53, line 10.

(10) Variable Labor. From Income Projection on page 53, line 9.

(11) Advertising. Budgeted at $400/month for the first year, plus an extra $600 in September for a tourist-oriented ad campaign and an extra $4,155 in April to an agency for the major wholesale marketing program, including implementation and execution.

(12) Insurance. Payable quarterly.

(13) Legal and Accounting. Payable quarterly.

(14) Delivery Expenses. Varies with volume of wholesale sales.

(15) Fixed Cash Disbursements. These are relatively independent of sales, so they are allocated evenly throughout the year. See display on lines (26) through (37) for details. If salaries fluctuate widely, break them out as a separate item with the other disbursements. For example, if you meet your payroll every other week, two months of the year will have three paydays rather than two, which can make those months look alarmingly costly.

(16) Mortgage (rent). Rent through December at $550/month, mortgage payments (principal and interest) at $876 thereafter.

(17) Term Loan. $535/month for seven years, which includes principal and interest.

(18) Line of Credit. Includes principal repayment and interest.

(19) Other.
    January: Purchase building
    March: Equipment purchase and building improvements to be paid in full.

(20) Total Cash Disbursements. Sum of lines (9) through (19).

(22) Net Cash Flow. (7) minus (20).

(24) Cumulative Cash Flow. (22) + last month's (24). This sums up the net cash flow on a monthly basis, adding the present month's net cash flow to last month's cumulative cash flow. This is useful on a periodic basis (monthly or quarterly). Over a longer time, it's of academic interest only.

Some experts advise pushing a cash flow until the cumulative cash flow is consistently positive.

(39)—(43) Cash Balance Reconciliation. (40) + (41) - (42) = (43). This display (for Year One only) may be used as a quick check on how well the budget is doing. For Years Two and Three, it is not accurate enough to be useful.

Notes and Explanations for
Finestkind Seafoods, Inc.
Cash Flow Projection by Month, Year One
Further explanation of these cash flow items appears on the
notes supporting the income projections, on pages 49 through 51.

(3) Sales Receivable. Our terms are cash retail, net 10 for wholesale accounts. Assumes 1/3 wholesale will turn to cash in the following month.

(4) Wholesale. See income projections for derivation of these figures.

(5) Retail. See income projections for derivation.

(6) Other Sources. October, November credit line, $7,500; January $75,000 mortgage and $30,000 new equity from Swan and Gosling; April term loan for improvements and equipment, $30,000; June inventory buildup, $15,000 from credit line.

(9) Cost of Goods. 72% of current month sales [line (6) of income projections].

(10) Variable Labor. Part-time help from May to September to handle extra weekend tourist trade and extra seafood preparation.

(11) Advertising. $1,000 initial burst, $400/month thereafter. Add $4,155 to April for wholesale marketing program.

(16) Mortgage. $550/month rent to December, mortgage payments January on. Terms: $75,000, 15 year, 11.5%.

(17) Term Loan. $534/month payments scheduled for term loan. Terms: $30,000, 7 year, 12.25%.

Cash Flow Projection by Month, Year One

#	A	B October	C November	D December	E January	F February	G March	H April	I May	J June	K July	L August	M September	N Total
1		October	November	December	January	February	March	April	May	June	July	August	September	Total
2	**Cash Receipts**													
3	Sales Receivable	$2,000	$1,350	$1,350	$1,750	$1,850	$2,000	$2,300	$2,300	$2,800	$3,500	$3,750	$3,750	$28,700
4	Wholesale	$2,650	$2,650	$3,450	$3,750	$4,000	$4,700	$4,700	$5,600	$7,100	$7,550	$7,550	$6,400	$60,100
5	Retail	$9,730	$9,500	$9,500	$9,000	$8,400	$8,750	$10,300	$11,540	$12,165	$12,165	$12,475	$12,475	$126,000
6	Other Sources (see notes)	$7,500	$7,500		$105,000			$30,000		$15,000				$165,000
7	**Total Cash Receipts:**	$21,880	$21,000	$14,300	$119,500	$14,250	$15,450	$47,300	$19,440	$37,065	$23,215	$23,775	$22,625	$379,800
8	**Cash Disbursements**													$0
9	Cost of Goods	$9,885	$9,720	$10,584	$10,512	$10,368	$11,340	$12,456	$14,357	$16,391	$16,895	$17,118	$15,894	$155,520
10	Variable Labor									$604	$796	$796	$604	$2,800
11	Advertising	$1,000	$400	$400	$400	$400	$400	$4,555	$400	$400	$400	$400	$400	$9,555
12	Insurance		$300			$300			$300			$300		$1,200
13	Legal and Accounting			$375			$375			$375			$375	$1,500
14	Delivery Expenses	$75	$75	$75	$100	$75	$100	$150	$200	$200	$250	$250	$250	$1,800
15	Fixed Cash Disbursements*	$2,535	$2,535	$2,535	$2,535	$2,535	$2,535	$2,535	$2,535	$2,535	$2,535	$2,535	$2,540	$30,425
16	Mortgage (rent)	$550	$550	$550	$876	$876	$876	$876	$876	$876	$876	$876	$876	$9,534
17	Term Loan							$534	$534	$534	$534	$534	$534	$3,204
18	Line of Credit		$85	$15,085						$165	$165	$15,000		$30,500
19	Other (see notes)				$105,000		$30,000							$135,000
20	**Total Cash Disbursements:**	$14,045	$13,665	$29,604	$119,423	$14,554	$45,626	$21,106	$19,202	$22,080	$22,451	$37,809	$21,473	$381,038
21	**Net Cash Flow:**	$7,835	$7,335	($15,304)	$77	($304)	($30,176)	$26,194	$238	$14,985	$764	($14,034)	$1,152	($1,238)
22														
23														
24	**Cumulative Cash Flow:**	$7,835	$15,170	($134)	($57)	($361)	($30,537)	($4,343)	($4,105)	$10,880	$11,644	($2,390)	($1,238)	
25														
26	*Fixed Cash Disbursements	(FCD)												
27	Utilities	$2,160												
28	Salaries	$22,800												
29	Payroll Taxes and Benefits	$2,850												
30	Office Supplies	$300												
31	Maintenance and Cleaning	$300												
32	Licenses	$115												
33	Boxes, Paper, etc.	$400												
34	Telephone	$1,020												
35	Miscellaneous	$480												
36	Total: FCD/yr	$30,425												
37	FCD/mo	$2,535												
38														
39	**Cash on Hand**													
40	Opening Balance	$2,150	$9,905	$17,240	$1,936	$2,013	$1,709	($28,467)	($2,273)	($2,035)	$12,950	$13,714	($320)	
41	+ Cash Receipts	$21,800	$21,000	$14,300	$119,500	$14,250	$15,450	$47,300	$19,440	$37,065	$23,215	$23,775	$22,625	$379,800
42	- Cash Disbursements	$14,045	$13,665	$29,604	$119,423	$14,554	$45,626	$21,106	$19,202	$22,080	$22,451	$37,809	$21,473	$381,038
43	Total = New Balance	$9,905	$17,240	$1,936	$2,013	$1,709	($28,467)	($2,273)	($2,035)	$12,950	$13,714	($320)	$832	

This spreadsheet was prepared using the Excel spreadsheet program from Microsoft.®

Notes and Explanations for
Finestkind Seafoods, Inc.
Cash Flow Projection by Quarters
for Years Two and Three

(4) Receivables turn from September, Year One. Since this is a quarterly summary, no further allowance will be made for receivables turn.

(7) Other Sources. $12,000 for one month on line of credit third quarter, $15,000 for nine weeks on line of credit fourth quarter to meet inventory needs.

(16) Fixed Cash Disbursements. Could have included mortgage and term loan payments, but to preserve parity with detail of Year One, loan payments are displayed separately.

(24) Cumulative Cash Flow. Subtract $1,238 from net cash flow, first quarter Year Two, to reflect the total cumulative cash flow of Year One: ($1,238).

(26) Fixed Cash Disbursements. From Income Projections.

You should notice that only the most important cash flow items are annotated. Such annotation helps you remember your thinking at some late time—and helps avoid repeating errors. It also makes your projections much more believable, since the numbers will be seen to have more foundation than guesswork.

Application of Funds Statement

This is a handy addition to your cash flow analysis. Your banker may be interested in a Source and Applications statement, which is a slightly more formal version—ask your CPA—but this is handy when you are looking at ways of financing major acquisitions.

Use of Funds	Total Amount Required:	From Equity:	From Loans:	From Other:
Acquire building	$105,000	$30,000	$75,000	
Improve building	24,000		20,000	$4,000
Equipment	10,000		10,000	

Cash Flow Projection by Quarter, Year Two

	A	B	C	D	E	F
1		1st Quarter	2nd Quarter	3rd Quarter	4th Quarter	Total
2	Cash Receipts					
3	Receivables	$3,200				$3,200
4	Wholesale	$38,900	$54,800	$76,500	$94,800	$265,000
5	Retail	$41,000	$37,400	$48,600	$53,000	$180,000
6	Other Sources			$12,000	$15,000	$27,000
7	Total Cash Receipts:	$83,100	$92,200	$137,100	$162,800	$475,200
8	Cash Disbursements					
9	Cost of Goods	$57,528	$66,384	$90,072	$106,416	$320,400
10	Variable Labor			$604	$2,196	$2,800
11	Advertising	$2,000	$2,305	$3,125	$3,695	$11,125
12	Insurance	$950	$950	$950	$950	$3,800
13	Legal and Accounting	$500	$500	$500	$500	$2,000
14	Delivery Expenses	$1,600	$1,844	$2,500	$2,956	$8,900
15	*Fixed Cash Disbursements	$12,630	$12,640	$12,640	$12,640	$50,550
16	Mortage (rent)	$2,628	$2,628	$2,628	$2,628	$10,512
17	Term Loan	$1,602	$1,602	$1,602	$1,602	$6,408
18	Line of Credit			$12,140	$15,360	$27,500
19	Other (see notes)					
20	Total Cash Disbursements:	$79,438	$88,853	$126,761	$148,943	$443,995
21						
22	Net Cash Flow:	$3,662	$3,347	$10,339	$13,857	$31,205
23						
24	Cumulative Cash Flow:	$2,424	$5,771	$16,110	$29,967	$54,272
25						
26	*Fixed Cash Disbursements					
27	(FCD)	Year Two				
28	Utilities	$2,640				
29	Salaries	$39,000				
30	Payroll Taxes and Benefits	$4,875				
31	Office Supplies	$360				
32	Maintenance and Cleaning	$360				
33	Licenses	$115				
34	Boxes, Paper, etc.	$800				
35	Telephone	$1,800				
36	Miscellaneous	$600				
37	Total: FCD/yr	$50,550				
38	FCD/qtr	$12,638				

This spreadsheet was prepared using the Excel spreadsheet program from Microsoft.®

Cash Flow Projection by Quarter, Year Three

	A	B	C	D	E	F
1		1st Qtr.	2nd Qtr.	3rd Qtr.	4th Qtr.	Total
2	Cash Receipts					
3	Receivables					$325,000
4	Wholesale	$58,750	$55,000	$97,500	$113,750	$325,000
5	Retail	$47,400	$43,600	$56,000	$63,000	$210,000
6	Other Sources			$12,000	$15,000	$27,000
7	Total Cash Receipts:	$106,150	$98,600	$165,500	$191,750	$562,000
8	Cash Disbursements					
9	Cost of Goods	$76,428	$70,992	$110,520	$127,260	$385,200
10	Variable Labor			$1,622	$5,898	$7,520
11	Advertising	$2,655	$2,465	$3,835	$4,420	$13,375
12	Insurance	$1,025	$1,025	$1,025	$1,025	$4,100
13	Legal and Accounting	$625	$625	$625	$625	$2,500
14	Delivery Expenses	$1,805	$1,675	$2,610	$3,010	$9,100
15	*Fixed Cash Disbursements	$15,215	$15,215	$15,215	$15,220	$60,865
16	Mortgage (rent)	$2,628	$2,628	$2,628	$2,628	$10,512
17	Term Loan	$1,602	$1,602	$1,602	$1,602	$6,408
18	Line of Credit			$12,140	$15,360	$27,500
19	Other (see notes)					
20	Total Cash Disbursements:	$101,983	$96,227	$151,822	$177,048	$527,080
21						
22	Net Cash Flow:	$4,167	$2,373	$13,678	$14,702	$34,920
23						
24	Cumulative Cash Flow:	$2,424	$4,797	$18,475	$33,177	$58,873
25						
26	*Fixed Cash Disbursement					
27	(FCD)	Year Three				
28	Utilities	$2,880				
29	Salaries	$46,800				
30	Payroll Taxes and Benefits	$5,850				
31	Office Supplies	$480				
32	Maintenance and Cleaning	$420				
33	Licenses	$115				
34	Boxes, Paper, etc.	$1,200				
35	Telephone	$2,400				
36	Miscellaneous	$720				
37	Total: FCD/yr	$60,865				
38	FCD/qtr	$15,216				

This spreadsheet was prepared using the Excel spreadsheet program from Microsoft.®

Appendix Two

Resources for Small Businesses

Resources for Small Businesses

There are many excellent texts available on small business management, but most are more appropriate for businesses with more than 100 employees. Check out your local library, college bookstores and these sources of small business management information:

Upstart Publishing Company, Inc. These publications on proven management techniques for small businesses are available from Upstart Publishing Company, Inc., 12 Portland Street, Dover, NH 03820. For a free current catalogue, call 800-235-8866 outside New Hampshire or 749-5071 in state.

- *Managing by the Numbers: Financial Essentials for the Growing Business,* © 1990, David H. Bangs Jr. and Upstart Publishing Company, Inc. This book makes financial management simple for the small business owner. It provides straightforward techniques for getting maximum return with a minimum of detail. Includes anecdotes, examples, case histories, forms and worksheets. (Softcover, 150 pages, $19.95)†

- *Creating Customers: An Action Plan for Maximizing Sales, Promotion and Publicity for the Small Business,* © 1990, Upstart Publishing Company, Inc. This is a book for business owners and managers who want a step-by-step approach to selling and promoting more successfully. Contains hundreds of techniques that business owners can apply *today*. (Softcover, 160 pages, $14.95)†

- *The Start Up Guide: A One-Year Plan for Entrepreneurs,* © 1989, David H. Bangs Jr. and Upstart Publishing Company, Inc. This book utilizes the same step-by-step, no-jargon method as the *Business Planning Guide* to assist those with no formal training through the process of beginning a successful business. (Softcover, 150 pages, $18.95)†

- *On Your Own: A Woman's Guide to Building a Business,* © 1990, Laurie Zuckerman, and Upstart Publishing Company, Inc. *On Your Own* is for women who want hands-on, practical information about starting and running a business. It deals honestly with issues like finding time for your business when you're also the primary care provider, societal biases against women and credit discrimination. (Softcover, 224 pages, $18.95)†

- *Buy the Right Business—At the Right Price,* © 1990, Brian Knight and the Associates of Country Business, Inc. and Upstart Publishing Company, Inc. Many people who would like to be in business for themselves think strictly of starting a business. In some cases, buying a going concern may be preferable—and just as affordable. (Softcover, 150 pages, $18.95)†

- *Market Planning Guide,* © 1987, 1989, 1990, David H. Bangs, Jr. and Upstart Publishing Company, Inc. A 150-page manual to help small-business owners put together a goal-oriented, resource-based marketing plan with action steps, benchmarks and timelines. Includes worksheets and checklists to make implementation and review easier. (Softcover, 150 pages, $18.95)†

- *Cash Flow Control Guide,* © 1987, 1990, David H. Bangs, Jr. and Upstart Publishing Company, Inc. A manual to help small-business owners solve their number-one financial problem. Includes worksheets and checklists. (Softcover, 70 pages, $10.95)†

†See page 71 for order form.

- *Personnel Planning Guide*, © 1986, 1987, 1988, 1990, David H. Bangs, Jr. and Upstart Publishing Company, Inc. A 160-page manual outlining practical and proven personnel management techniques, including hiring, managing, evaluating and compensating personnel. Includes worksheets and checklists. (Softcover, 160 pages, $18.95)†

- *The Business Planning Guide*, © 1976, 1985, 1989, 1990, David H. Bangs, Jr. and Upstart Publishing Company, Inc. A 150-page manual that helps you write a business plan and financing proposal tailored to your business, your goals and your resources. Includes worksheets and checklists. (Softcover, 150 pages, $18.95)†

Small Business Reporter. An excellent series of booklets on small-business management published by Bank of America, Department 3120, PO Box 37000, San Francisco, CA 94137 (415) 622-2491. Individual copies are $5 each. Ask for a list of current titles—they have about 17 available, including *Steps to Starting a Business, Avoiding Management Pitfalls, Business Financing* and *Marketing Small Business*.

In Business. A bimonthly magazine for small businesses, especially those with less than 10 employees. The publisher is J.G. Press, PO Box 323, Emmaus, PA 18049. Annual subscriptions are $18.

The Great Brain Robbery, Ray Considine and Murray Raphel, © 1980, 1981, by The Great Brain Robbery, 1360 East Rubio Street, Altadena, CA 91101. Subtitled "A collection of proven ideas to make you money and change your life!," *The Great Brain Robbery* contains numerous checklists and ideas which are thought-provoking. The chapters entitled "Formula for Success," "Secret Selling Sentences" and "If You Don't Like It Here, Get Out!" are particularly provocative. Raphel and Considine are marketing and promotional experts—which is apparent throughout this book.

Marketing with Facts, © 1986, published by Price Waterhouse, 1251 Avenue of the Americas, New York, NY 10020. This book, part of a series aimed at small-business owners and entrepreneurs, focuses on how marketing information can be used to enhance opportunities for profit. The book's lists of questions and lexicon of marketing terminology are particularly helpful. Copies of this book cost $5.00 and are available at any Price Waterhouse office.

Other Tools for Small-Business Owners

Software for small businesses. The best integrated planning package for small-business owners we've come across is Plans 'n Totals™, which requires an IBM PC or equivalent with 512K RAM. Plans 'n Totals™ provides menus to help prepare financial projections and budgets, and then helps you analyze them (break-even and ratio analysis are built in). Call 617-264-4450, or write to Resource N Corporation, 721 Lowell Road, Carlisle, MA 01741 for current price information. A demo disk is available.

Financial Templates. PSI Research, 300 N. Valley Drive, Grants Pass, OR 97526 offers excellent financial templates for small-business owners. *Small Business Expert* is for use with IBM and compatibles and *Financial Templates for Small Business* is for use with Excel™ on the Macintosh.™ You may also find ready-made templates for specific business applications available from local computer clubs.

Additional Resources

Small Business Development Centers (SBDCs). Call your state university or the Small Business Administration (SBA) to find the SBDC nearest you. Far and away the best free management program available, SBDCs provide expert assistance and training in every aspect of business management. Don't ignore this resource.

SCORE, or Service Corps of Retired Executives, sponsored by the U.S. Small Business Administration, provides free counseling and also a series of workshops and seminars for small businesses. Of special interest: SCORE offers a Business Planning Workshop which includes a 30-minute video produced specifically for SCORE by Upstart Publishing and funded by Paychex, Inc. There are over 500 SCORE chapters nationwide. For more information, contact the SBA office nearest you and ask about SCORE.

Small Business Administration (SBA). The SBA offers a number of management assistance programs. If you are assigned a capable Management Assistance Officer, you have an excellent resource. The SBA is worth a visit, if only to leaf through their extensive literature.

Colleges and universities. Most have business courses. Some have SBDCs, others have more specialized programs. Some have small-business expertise—the University of New Hampshire, for example, has two schools which provide direct small-business management assistance.

Keye Productivity Center, P.O. Box 23192, Kansas City, MO 64141. Keye Productivity offers business seminars on specific personnel topics for a reasonable fee. Call them at 800-821-3919 for topics and prices. Their seminar entitled *Hiring and Firing* is excellent, well-documented and useful. Good handout materials are included.

Comprehensive Accounting Corporation, 2111 Comprehensive Drive, Aurora, IL 60507. CAC has over 425 franchised offices providing accounting, bookkeeping and management consulting services to small businesses. For information, call 800-323-9009.

Center for Entrepreneurial Management, 29 Greene Street, New York, NY 10013. The oldest and largest nonprofit membership association for small-business owners in the world. They maintain an extensive list of books, videotapes, cassettes and other small-business management aids. Call 212-925-7304 for information.

Libraries. Do not forget to take advantage of the information readily available at your library.